Burslem Campus

Stoke on Trent Learning Resources Centre
College

4 Week Loan

Telephone:

01782 603142

Please return or renew by the date stamped below

WITHDRAWN

PERFECT
CPD

Teacher-Led

Shaun Allison Edited by Jackie Beere

 Independent Thinking Press

First published by
Independent Thinking Press
Crown Buildings, Bancyfelin, Carmarthen, Wales, SA33 5ND, UK
www.independentthinkingpress.com

Independent Thinking Press is an imprint of Crown House Publishing Ltd.

First published 2014

British Library Cataloguing-in-Publication Data
A catalogue entry for this book is available
from the British Library.

Print ISBN 978-178135136-9
Mobi ISBN 978-178135196-3
ePub ISBN 978-178135197-0
ePDF ISBN 978-178135198-7

Printed and bound in the UK by
Gomer Press, Llandysul, Ceredigion

Contents

Acknowledgements

I have been fortunate enough to work with a number of excellent school leaders and teachers over the years, many of whom have influenced what I have written about in this book – so thank you all. I would like to thank two people in particular who have influenced, supported and encouraged me in recent years.

Firstly, Sue Marooney, my current head teacher at Durrington High School and friend. Sue is an inspiration to all, with the most remarkable vision, drive and ambition for school improvement. Her commitment to excellence for every young person is unswerving. Secondly, my deputy head colleague and friend, Jane Squires. Jane is brilliant. She just gets it! Everything! Sue and Jane have been a huge support to me and I cannot thank them enough. I am incredibly fortunate to have them as friends and colleagues.

My gorgeous wife, Lianne, and my four wonderful children, May, Finn, Eve and Jude, continue to inspire me and make me smile every day. Lastly, of course, a huge thank you to my lovely mother, Joyce Allison, who always told me that school was important!

Shaun Allison **@shaun_allison**

Foreword

A school is only as good as its teachers. With the relentless focus in recent years on teaching and learning, as well as outcomes, this has never been more true. It has led us all to think in new ways about how to improve the classroom experience for children – and teachers. It is teachers who make the difference to children's life chances, so the quest to get more good and outstanding teachers in front of children is a key challenge for all school leaders.

One of the most crucial – and most rewarding – jobs in a school is to be in charge of teacher training and development, encouraging individuals to continue to learn and grow. This book has been written by someone who has been doing that very job with flair, enthusiasm and passion, and it seeps through every page. It is full of very practical ideas to create a culture in your school where every member of staff becomes continuously curious about learning and engaged in action research about what works best to help our learners. After all, putting teachers in charge of their own development is at the heart of great school leadership.

Continuing professional development has changed radically in the last ten years. Genuine collaborative learning is taking place via TeachMeets (where teachers from various schools share real classroom experiences), learning visits to other schools, learning forums, research projects and peer coaching, all of which are becoming increasingly integral to staff development. School leaders are also taking performance management procedures from being an over-formal paper exercise to being a live, ongoing process that really contributes to continuous improvement. CPD has started to become an essential part of the staffroom culture.

As teachers, we often breathe a metaphorical sigh of relief after the first few tough years of teaching. Suddenly we don't have to submit all our lesson plans, get regular observation assessments or write that research piece to gain accreditation. However, we sometimes need to be reminded that the real challenges in our careers often come just when we think the students know us well, when we've finally got the schemes of work cracked and so begin to believe that we don't have to work quite so hard. Shaun highlights research evidence which shows that, after the first three years of intense development, improvement can plateau. He argues that this is exactly when training and development, as part of a whole-school culture, will make the difference between a school that 'requires improvement' and one that is continually improving.

Many schools would benefit from a comprehensive guide to making CPD *really* deliver staff improvement – and this is exactly what Shaun has produced. He describes a mix-and-match approach that offers real, individualised development, which is actually owned by the teachers and anchored firmly in the values and vision of the school. It couldn't be more relevant, at a time when teachers are leaving the profession because of the pressures of a constantly changing agenda and what feels like relentless political interference.

Schools have the chance to seize the day and take control of their own journey towards improvement. Whatever your school type, phase or location, there are gems here that will inspire you to create CPD that works.

Good luck!

Jackie Beere, Tiffield

Introduction

Schools are enigmatic. They are complex communities that are both unique and similar. Mission statements will vary from school to school but ultimately they all have the same aim: to produce happy, confident and successful young people. So, the key question has to be, why are some schools better at doing this than others? School cohorts, local communities and buildings may differ, as may resources, the use of innovative technologies, class sizes and a whole range of other factors. However, the very best schools all have two things in common: great leadership and a large number of great teachers. The very best schools, then, have a relentless focus on making sure that even more of their teachers become great.

> [T]he main reason that most system-wide educational reforms have failed is that they have ignored (1) the importance of teacher quality for student progress; (2) the fact that it is highly variable; and (3) that teacher quality has differential impact on different students.
>
> Wiliam (2010: 1)

There is much research evidence to back up this assertion, but anyone who has worked in schools for any length of time will know that there is a direct correlation between the success of a particular school and the number of talented teachers in the staffroom. What do these great teachers look like? Well, while preparing a leaving speech for a very well-respected colleague recently, I asked Andrew, a Year 8 student, what made my colleague such a great teacher. His response summed it up brilliantly:

> He likes us, makes it fun, but still makes us work really hard and expects us to do well. He's much cleverer than some of the other science teachers, but still makes it easy to learn. He lets us know how we're doing.

I know the teacher that Andrew describes very well and this is spot on. His lessons are always a joy to observe and he consistently secures very strong outcomes for his students. We know that teachers like this make a positive difference to students and that the more teachers there are like this in a school, the better the school. Unfortunately, evidence suggests that after two or three years of teaching, most teachers start to plateau in terms of their classroom performance. Why? Well, being a new teacher is difficult and you have to sharpen your classroom skills very quickly if you are going to survive. Once you have mastered the basic skills to 'get by' in the classroom, the temptation is to sit back a bit. Alongside this, most new teachers have a mentor working with them, giving feedback on their performance and helping them to improve. In most schools, this support is not available beyond the first year of teaching. However, without feedback, performance is unlikely to improve.

Teaching has become a very pressured and much-scrutinised profession. However, I still believe very strongly that it is one of the best jobs in the world. Nothing gives me greater professional satisfaction than a teacher coming to talk to me about a new teaching strategy they have tried out in their classroom that has gone well, and which they want to develop further and share with colleagues. To me, this is what the job of school leadership is about – creating a spark that lights little individual fires of great pedagogy around the school, which then gather momentum and become an inferno of excellence! In order to do this, the continuing professional development (CPD) leader needs to:

- Get teachers excited about teaching.
- Get teachers talking about teaching.
- Get teachers planning and evaluating their teaching together.
- Get teachers observing and learning from each other.
- Get teachers sharing what works with each other.

> I love a challenge, and there are few things better than celebrating others overcoming challenges.
>
> Richard Branson, **@richardbranson** (15 August 2013)

In their book, *Switch: How to Change Things When Change is Hard* (2011), Chip and Dan Heath describe what successful institutions do: they find what is working and do more of it. They refer to this as 'finding the bright spots'. This simple but very important idea is the principle behind this book – find the bright spots in your school, that is the great teachers, and share what they are doing. Furthermore, find the bright spots from outside your school and bring them into your school.

This book aims to give you some ideas about how a range of CPD opportunities can be set up within your school to light your own fires of great pedagogy.

Chapter 1

Why Teachers Matter – Why CPD Matters

In his book, *Outliers: The Story of Success* (2008), Malcolm Gladwell suggests that it takes about 10,000 hours to become an 'expert' at a particular skill. For teachers, this amounts to about ten years of classroom practice. Now, the accuracy of the 10,000 hours as a definitive timeline for achieving expertise in teaching is open for discussion. However, very few of us would argue against the fact that the very best teachers refine their skills over a number of years, and certainly beyond the second or third year of their careers. However, as discussed in the Introduction, most will plateau at this point and just stick with 'what they've always done' in the classroom. This presents us with a problem. If most teachers stop getting better after two or three years, whereas in fact they should be developing their skills over ten years in order to reach an 'expert' level, what should we be doing as school leaders to address this 'professional development deficit'?

The answer to this problem is relatively straightforward. We need to give staff a range of CPD opportunities that will engage, enthuse and motivate them. By this, I don't just mean the traditional model of courses and INSET days – sat in a hall and listening to an 'expert' who hasn't stepped inside a school for years. I mean a rich and varied ongoing programme of activities that staff can engage with on a number of levels and which will support them to reflect upon and develop their own practice. Teachers are the most important asset in a school, so they should be professionally developed and nurtured in a way that interests and inspires them.

As well as providing CPD opportunities, we also need to develop a culture within schools of 'continuous improvement'. This means a school where teachers want to take risks (and feel safe in doing so), seek and try out new ideas and strategies, and discuss their work openly. It's a school where teachers are happy and positively thrive on collaborating with and learning from each other. Providing CPD opportunities to facilitate this collaboration is the starting point. The best indicator that you're on the right path is when it's happening informally and frequently – at breaktime, in the corridors and by the kettle in the staffroom.

School leaders need to think about how they will achieve this within their schools. A successful CPD model uses a layered approach in which three distinct strands of CPD are operating.

A layered approach to CPD

BLANKET

Important development work that all teachers need to be involved in and which aligns with whole-school improvement priorities

Delivered through: INSET days, staff meetings, appraisal, etc.

OPTIONAL

A range of developmental activities that teachers can opt into, with a view to personalising their CPD and so allowing them to follow their own interests

Delivered through: 15 minute forums, IRIS observations, lesson study, peer observations, action research, coaching, school visits, etc.

DIRECTED

When staff are underperforming they are directed to engage in specific developmental, support work

Delivered through: mentoring and coaching

This approach ensures that everyone experiences the same CPD and aligns their practice with the whole-school vision, while also providing opportunities for those who want to engage at a deeper level. It also addresses the issue of underperformance. The school leadership team then needs to be committed to putting in place a range of creative activities to fill in the layers using the expertise that exists within the school. The CPD needs of any school can be met by the good practice that is already present within it. It's just a case of seeking it out and using a variety of mechanisms to share it – and, in doing so, inspiring others.

In order to do this effectively, school leaders need to ask themselves a number of key questions:

- Does your school have a shared understanding of what great teaching looks like?

- Do you actively encourage all teachers to engage in an ongoing cycle of reflection and improvement?

- Do leaders within the school (at all levels) discuss teaching and learning and how to make it better?

- Do you know who your best teachers are? Do you know why they are so good?

- Do you know who your weakest teachers are? Are you supporting them to get better?

- Do you provide opportunities for other teachers to learn from these expert teachers?

- Do you have a range of CPD opportunities that staff can engage with and that allow them to learn from each other?

- Do you encourage your teachers to seek best practice from other schools and then bring those ideas into your school?

- Do you provide opportunities for teachers to follow their own professional development priorities?

- Do you provide the opportunities for your teachers to engage in action research?
- Do you expect all of your teachers to strive for excellence in the classroom?

Working through this series of questions would be a good 'health check' for a school leadership team. Developing the quality of teaching and learning with a view to reducing any within-school variation should be the number one priority for any school leadership team. A varied and innovative CPD programme is the answer to achieving this.

> The most distinctive feature in the schools visited was the commitment of leaders at all levels to using professional development as the main vehicle for bringing about improvement. All had a clear view of how professional development should be organised.
>
> Ofsted (2010: 7)

The first question, whether your school has a shared understanding of what great teaching looks like, is fundamental. It's important to know what works and develop this across the school. In his book, *The Six Secrets of Change*, Michael Fullan describes the importance of this approach:

> The intent is to define the best methods for reducing variation in favour of practices that are known to be effective, identifying the few key practices that are crucial to success.
>
> Fullan (2008: 79)

It is important for teachers and senior leaders to spend time discussing what great teaching looks like in their school. At my own school, we have distilled what we think great teaching is about into four distinct areas of pedagogy, or 'The Big 4':

1. Questioning – ask deep, probing questions that encourage and support thinking.

2. Feedback – ensure students get feedback that is specific, helpful and helps to close the learning gap.

3. Independence – teaching should provide students with the confidence and tools to tackle problems with less dependence on the teacher, through explanation, modelling, discussion and practice.

4. Challenge – students of all abilities should be challenged to get better and better.

The very best teachers are skilled in these four areas, so it seems perfectly sensible that these should be the areas of pedagogy we should be looking to develop in *all* teachers. As teaching is a creative profession, we adopt a 'tight but loose' approach to our expectations: tight because these four areas of pedagogy should be strong features of teaching in all lessons, but loose because teachers can choose to implement them in a variety of ways – as long as it works. As a list, it is also very easy to remember, so there is more chance of it having an impact than a long list of criteria that will be easily forgotten.

Once a shared understanding is in place within a school, the CPD programme should then flow from it. In my school, the CPD programme is focused on developing 'The Big 4' with all teachers – with the emphasis on *all*. In your school it may well be something quite different. The challenge for school CPD leaders is to put together a varied and robust CPD programme that will allow teachers to engage with your priorities and at a level with which they feel comfortable. It's about making sure that all teachers are encouraged to at least try out a few new strategies, while others have the opportunity to take their own personal development further and deeper.

The energy and excitement that came out of the 2012 London Olympics is hard to forget. One of the most successful GB teams was the cycling team, headed up by coach Dave Brailsford. The success of the team was put down largely to the idea of 'marginal gains' – looking at every aspect of cycling and making slight improvements. The idea is that the combined effect of these small improvements will result in a big overall improvement in performance. The same theory can, of course, be applied to teaching using an effective CPD programme. By making small adjustments to our practice, we can make a big difference to the learning of our students. A simple but highly effective idea.

So, what do teachers want in terms of CPD? To answer this question, I asked teachers and school leaders on Twitter to finish this sentence: 'The best CPD is …' Here are some of their responses:

- Matched to individual and/or institution priorities.
- Encouraging teachers to talk about teaching to teachers.
- Informed by evidence.
- Challenging.
- Learning from each other.
- Personalised but also builds the professional capital of the school.
- Sustained, learning-focused, teacher-driven, evaluated, collaborative and challenging.
- Like good feedback – specific, positive and developmental.
- Ongoing – not a day course but lots of chances to meet up and discuss/reflect on practice.
- Chosen by you, not done to you.

- That which you seek for yourself – learning comes from within.
- Sharing good practice that is working in your classroom with others, by talking to each other.
- Shared peer-to-peer by practitioners, not delivered from on high by 'consultants'.
- Something that addresses a need you have, so that you actually benefit from it and then others can benefit from it too.
- Paired with the opportunity to go away, try whatever the CPD was about, then meet up with a partner at a future date to reflect and discuss.
- Done by those who do, day in, day out, and not by those who charge by the hour.
- Encouraging risk taking in the pursuit of great teaching.
- Like the best lessons – differentiated according to need, with some variety and discussion time.
- Practical, so it can have a positive impact in the classroom.
- Learning from doing and is based on sound research.

For me, two very clear principles regarding teacher CPD emerge from this list:

1. Teachers are highly reflective when it comes to their own practice and want to be the best that they possibly can be.

2. Teachers want to progress by working alongside their peers to learn from best practice.

In terms of an Ofsted judgement, the importance of using CPD to improve the quality of teaching in a school is clear. The 2014 *School Inspection Handbook* suggests that inspectors will assess 'how professional development has improved the quality of teaching', 'the extent to which leaders' monitoring of teaching has identified needs and provided targeted pedagogical guidance and support for teachers' and 'the nature and impact of performance management' (Ofsted, 2014: 13).

Ofsted also considers the role of performance management in assessing the success of a school's professional development:

> The survey schools' arrangements for performance management played a major role in determining the content of their professional development. They had rigorous systems which helped to identify priorities at individual, subject, faculty and whole-institution level.
>
> Ofsted (2010: 9)

In terms of appraisal, schools are expected to:

- Set clear objectives for all teachers, relevant to their career stage and linked to the *Teachers' Standards*.
- Put in place appropriate CPD to support teachers with achieving these objectives.

■ Monitor and evaluate the impact of this CPD and the progress made towards meeting these objectives.

It is important that appraisal is seen as a continual and ongoing process which is linked to school and personal improvement and growth. It should not be a one-off, paper-work-driven process. Consequently, it is essential that schools have in place a varied and effective CPD programme that will enable all teachers to grow and develop professionally – and, in doing so, meet their appraisal objectives.

As an institution, it is worth reflecting on how well aligned your appraisal and CPD systems and processes are. The following questions might help:

■ Do you provide time for appraisers and appraisees to meet, so that they can have dialogues about their objectives for the year?

■ Are discussions about CPD an integral part of the appraisal process? For example, in the objective-setting table overleaf, the 'Evidence and action' column makes it explicit that CPD should be discussed and planned.

■ Do appraisers receive appropriate training that makes them aware of the CPD opportunities available for staff?

■ When whole-school CPD is taking place (e.g. coaching), are staff reminded to link this back to their appraisal objectives?

■ Do you make time throughout the year for appraisal objectives to be reviewed, so that CPD actions can also be reviewed and updated?

Objective What do you want to achieve?		Evidence and action 1. What evidence will be used to demonstrate this success? 2. What actions and CPD will you undertake to support this development?
1. Progress and outcomes		
2. Teaching and learning	Standard: 2	
	Standards: 1, 2, 3, 4, 5, 6, 7, 8 (circle appropriate standard/s)	
3. Personal leadership development	Standards: 1, 2, 3, 4, 5, 6, 7, 8 (circle appropriate standard/s)	

■ Do you give your staff access to a range of CPD activities, so that they can engage in CPD that will meet their personal needs?

The purpose of this book is to describe, in a very practical way, a variety of tried and tested CPD strategies that schools could choose to implement. Hopefully, school leaders will be able to treat it as a pick 'n' mix to support them with shaping their own CPD programme. Most of the strategies discussed in this book can work either at a whole-school level or at a subject level, to develop subject specific pedagogy.

The following five aspects will be covered for each CPD strategy:

1. A *description* of the strategy.

2. How it was *implemented* successfully (and how problems were overcome).

3. An *evaluation* of the strategy.

4. *Stay connected* – once you have implemented strategies, how you can use Twitter hashtags to share your experiences and find out about others' experiences.

5. *To-do list* – a short summary of what you need to do if you are going to implement the strategy.

Chapter 2

15 Minute Forums

Description

One of the most effective CPD strategies that can be set up in a school is the 15 minute forum. The original idea was conceived at Boundstone Community College (in Lancing, West Sussex) by an advanced skills teacher, John McKee. The idea is very simple: to set up a regular time slot during the school week when teachers can meet to share good ideas and resources.

Forums work best if they take place at the same time and on the same day every week (in my current school they are held every Thursday from 3.30–3.45 p.m.). Ideally, they should be informal and simply hosted in a classroom. Each session is led by a colleague who is willing to share a successful teaching strategy and/or resource that they have used in their own classroom. They present for five to ten minutes. This is then followed by a brief discussion about the strategy/resource during which other colleagues have the opportunity to describe similar strategies or resources. After 15 minutes of pedagogical patter, the session ends and the attendees go off to get on with their other work.

Implementation

For 15 minute forums to be really successful, they need to be led by classroom teachers talking about their own professional journeys. This gives them far more credibility than senior leaders pronouncing on what they think teaching should be like! So, the first issue to contend with is finding suitable and willing teachers to lead the sessions.

There is really only one way to do this: identify your best teachers and then approach them. This is where your skills of persuasion/arm-twisting/bribery will come into play! In my experience, the majority of teachers are very coy when it comes to talking to their peers about what they do in the classroom. With this in mind, they will need gentle and careful persuasion to lead a session. This is particularly difficult when you are starting off this initiative, as they won't know what to expect. However, as the programme gathers momentum and people see how the forums work and their value, they will become more willing to get involved. In the early days, I had to spend a lot of time each week persuading people to do a 15 minute forum once a fortnight. This is now very different and people are much more willing to step up.

To start with, it is recommended that you select teachers who are well respected by their peers – and not senior leaders. These are the teachers who do a great job every day, get good results and are well liked by the staff. This will encourage other people to come along, as they will be interested to hear what their esteemed colleague has to say. Once you have a good initial programme up and running, with good attendance figures, you can then begin to approach those attending to lead a session.

Another way to recruit forum leaders is by simply being on the ground and seeking out good practice in classrooms. This might be during an observation, a work scrutiny, a learning walk or simply a conversation about what teachers are doing in their classrooms. If it sounds interesting, ask them to lead a forum on it.

Once you have your 15 minute forum schedule planned out, the next issue is getting people to attend. As already mentioned, by carefully choosing people with credibility among the staff to lead the sessions, you will automatically attract a good number of attendees. At our school, we make it compulsory for all newly qualified teachers (NQTs) to attend all 15 minute forums – it is such a great opportunity for them not only to learn from their peers but also to meet other people in the school. As NQTs get further into their induction year, they are also encouraged to lead a forum.

Staff can be emailed the day before the forum to let them know what the topic is and who will be leading it. This information can also be published in the staff weekly bulletin (and mentioned in the whole-staff briefing), if you have one. It is also worth talking to your colleagues in the leadership team to encourage people in the subject areas they line

Here is an example of how a 15 minute forum programme might look:

Week 1	Questioning, Feedback, Independence and Challenge
Week 2	See It, Learn It!
Week 3	Developing Skills-Based Learning
Week 4	Using the 'Learning Journey' Poster Effectively
Week 5	Students as Bloggers
Week 6	Questioning Techniques
Week 7	Effective and Manageable Marking
Week 8	Developing Independence
Week 9	Demonstrating Progress in a Lesson
Week 10	Supporting the Progress of Low-Ability Students
Week 11	Using Socrative for Quick and Effective Assessment
Week 12	Developing Literacy Skills ... in All Subjects
Week 13	Using Questioning Effectively to Deepen Learning
Week 14	Closing the Marking/Feedback Loop
Week 15	Using Modelling to Develop Writing
Week 16	Talk for Writing
Week 17	Letting the Learning Run Itself
Week 18	Using Resources Effectively
Week 19	Alternatives to PowerPoint
Week 20	Ensuring Challenge and Success for All Learners in Lessons
Week 21	Using Video Clips Effectively

manage to attend. This is a good way of directing staff who need to develop a particular aspect of their work to come along – for example, if a marking walk has identified issues with a certain individual, they could be encouraged to attend a forum on marking.

After each forum, you might want to write up a summary of the shared strategies that have been discussed and send it to all staff via email. This idea can be further developed by setting up a blog where you can summarise each forum. This ensures that all staff can access the strategies at any time, while also opening it up to colleagues from schools all over the world. For example, our school CPD blog (http://classteaching.wordpress.com) has had 85,000 views to date.

Another option is to promote the topic for each weekly forum on Twitter. This enables colleagues from other schools to contribute to the forum, so widening the pool of good practice. A good way to do this is by using the website http://padlet.com. This is a great resource that allows you to set up a blank 'wall' to which anyone can contribute. So, you could set up a '15 minute forum' wall that anyone can post ideas to and which can then be shared during the forum.

Evaluation

There are many benefits to the 15 minute forum as a CPD strategy:

- Forums provide a regular opportunity to share the best practice that is happening throughout the school.
- The sessions act as a celebration of great teaching within the school.
- As the sessions are very short and to the point, they are not burdensome – after all, teachers are very busy people.
- It allows teachers to personalise their CPD by attending sessions that are relevant to their development priorities.
- They often act as a starting point for further developmental work (e.g. teachers sharing resources, observing each other, planning together, coaching each other).
- The informal nature of the sessions means that staff are more likely to open up and share their thoughts and ideas.

Stay connected

- Use the Twitter hashtag **#perfectcpd15mf** to share your experiences of 15 minute forums.

To-do list

- Find your best practitioners and ask them to lead a 15 minute forum. ☑

- Put a note out to all staff asking if anyone would like to lead a 15 minute forum. ☑

- Put together a programme of forums. ☑

- Distribute the programme to staff and publicise it at every opportunity. ☑

- Actively recruit people to attend. ☑

- Celebrate the successes of the forums with a view to encouraging more people to attend. ☑

Chapter 3

Coaching

Description

In terms of personalised CPD, it doesn't get much better than coaching. Coaching is a professional and supportive relationship, based on trust, between (usually) two colleagues. The purpose is for the coach to help the coachee to identify the solutions to their problems for themselves. Coaching is not about telling people how to get better – it is a solutions-focused approach based on asking directed questions. In this respect, it is different from mentoring. Mentoring usually involves a more experienced individual supporting a colleague by giving them advice and ideas about how to improve. Coaching is non-hierarchical and uses questioning to help people find their own solutions. Hence, mentoring is about input and coaching is about drawing out.

There are many models that can be used to help structure and shape a coaching conversation. The HILDA model (from *The Coaching Toolkit* (2009) by Shaun Allison and Michael

Harbour) provides a simple and focused framework to support the coach to ask the right questions:

- *Highlight* the issue. What issue does the coachee want to address? What do they want to be different and why?

- *Identify* the strengths. What do they already do well? How could these skills and attributes be used to address this particular issue?

- *Look* at the possibilities. In an ideal world, with no obstacles, what could they do to address the issues? What is getting in the way of doing this? How could these obstacles be overcome? What have they already tried? What worked and what didn't?

- *Decide* and commit to action. What are they going to do to address the issue? When are they going to do it? How are they going to do it? What support might they need and from whom?

- *Analyse* and evaluate the impact. How will they know if they have been successful? What will success look like?

Implementation

Coaching has huge potential in schools as a model of CPD. It is a great way of encouraging teachers to work collaboratively to support each other with improving their teaching or leadership. Furthermore, it can also be used by non-teaching staff in schools to improve their practice.

There are many different ways in which coaching can be implemented in schools.

1. *Group of coaches*. Schools can identify a group of teachers and invite them to train as coaches. If the coaches are to have credibility with their peers, they should be strong classroom practitioners. When selecting potential coaches, it is also worth considering the following characteristics of a good coach:

   - A good listener.
   - Able to ask open questions.
   - Good at summarising and clarifying points.
   - Encourages reflection.
   - Builds rapport easily.
   - Is non-judgemental.
   - Is confident in challenging beliefs.
   - Is able to see the big picture.
   - Is assertive when getting people to commit to an action.
   - Understands that they do not have all the answers.
   - Respects confidentiality.
   - Is solutions focused.
   - Holds a strong belief that colleagues have the capacity to improve.

In terms of training coaches, this doesn't have to be lengthy. The following process works well:

a. Discuss what coaching is and how it differs from mentoring.

b. Go through the HILDA model and the characteristics of a good coach.

c. Put the group into pairs (e.g. A and B).

d. A coaches B on an issue of their choosing, then B coaches A.

e. In pairs, discuss how the coaching went.

f. Pairs then feed back to the whole group. How did it feel to be coached/the coach? How was it different from other 'conversations' you may have had? What was easy/difficult about it? What have you learned from it, in terms of becoming an effective coach?

Once the coaches have had this initial training and are feeling confident, coaching can then be opened up to the staff. Let them know that there are coaching colleagues available that they can work with to develop their practice. The best approach is for interested staff to let the CPD coordinator (as this is usually the person responsible for setting up coaching in a school) know that they are interested in working with a coach. The CPD coordinator can then match them up with one of the coaches, who will then make contact with the teacher. It is then up to the pair to arrange any coaching sessions. As a rule, there should be at least three sessions, with time in between each one for the coachee to put into place the actions that have been agreed.

With this type of coaching, where colleagues are putting themselves forward to be coached, it works best if the process is paper free – there are no forms to fill in. It should simply be a professional, supportive conversation between two colleagues. However, it can be useful for the coaches to meet together to discuss and share any issues that have come up within the coaching. This also serves as an opportunity to further develop their own coaching skills.

2. *Coaching role.* Many schools now have a specific salaried role which is focused on coaching. At my school we call these skilled teachers 'learning leaders'. Through our own rigorous self-evaluation cycle, we identify teachers who require support in an area of their teaching. This will then be discussed with the teacher concerned, who will be assigned a learning leader to work with on that problem. The pair will then undertake an intensive coaching programme to address the issue that has been identified, usually over a period of six weeks.

By recruiting the right people as coaches, the school can become very effective in resolving professional difficulties that may arise among staff. Coaches need to be able to support teachers who have been told that there is an issue with their practice and then work through a series of quite normal responses:

- Denial – colleagues will often refuse to believe that there is a problem.
- Anger – denial often turns into anger ('Why me?').
- Withdrawal – as a result, they may then withdraw and not engage with the process.
- Acceptance – with a skilled and supportive coach, most will get to the point where they accept that coaching will be beneficial to them.

It takes someone who is relentless, focused and highly supportive to do the job well. But good coaches can effect a real transformation on teachers who are struggling with a particular area of their practice. Dealing with 'stuck' teachers is an ever more important issue for school leaders to address, so coaching could be part of the solution.

3. *Whole-school co-coaching*. With this approach the whole staff are given some preliminary coaching training and then put into pairs (or put themselves into pairs) to co-coach each other – so A coaches B and then B coaches A. You will need to decide the best 'pairing approach' for your school. By putting staff into pairs, you can control who coaches whom, based on individual strengths and weaknesses. Alternatively, by allowing people to pair themselves up, they can choose who they will feel most comfortable working with. However, there is the danger of the relationship between two friends just becoming a friendly chat, as opposed to a focused coaching conversation.

Following this, time can be set aside during INSET days and/or staff meetings for coaching pairs to meet and have a coaching conversation. It is very important that time is committed and set aside for coaching to happen. If it isn't then, in the vast majority of cases, the coaching probably won't happen. At the end of each session, it is important that each person in the pair commits to action and that this is reviewed at the next session.

There are clear advantages to engaging all teachers in coaching in this manner – in doing so, you are developing an ethos and culture where it is believed that we can all continue to learn and improve as teachers. As Carol Dweck asserts in her book, *Mindset: How You Can Fulfil Your Potential* (2006: 194), 'great teachers believe in the growth of the intellect and talent, and they are fascinated with the process of learning'.

Staff should be encouraged to keep their own coaching log as evidence for their CPD file. This can be a simple document that looks at, for example, identified issues to develop, agreed actions and a review of progress (to complete before the next coaching session).

4. *Specialist coaching.* Some schools identify an area of pedagogy that they want to develop across the school and then employ specialist coaches to lead and support teachers in it. For example, Angmering School, West Sussex, has appointed a team of 'e-coaches'. Their role is

to work alongside staff in a coaching capacity to develop their use of innovative technologies across the school.

Evaluation

Coaching offers a huge number of benefits for schools:

- When staff are able to solve their own problems by coaching, you are building capacity for future development. Problem solving is an important quality in school leaders.

- It develops a growth mindset. When staff feel more confident about solving their own issues, they are more likely to do so again, and so continue to develop and improve their own practice.

- When we feel that we are supported with developing our own practice and encouraged to try out new things, our self-esteem improves, which means we are more likely to take risks. Risk taking leads to innovation and the development of new and exciting teaching strategies.

- Because the coach works in the same context as the coachee, they understand the context of the issue, which makes it easier to help the coachee come up with an effective solution.

- As a culture of coaching grows within a school, individuals and groups get to the nub of an issue quickly, deal with it efficiently, improve it and then move on. Problems are less likely to linger or fester. When coaching is happening informally and frequently (also known as Martini coaching!), it becomes a very powerful tool for continuous improvement.

- Coaching fosters team spirit because it is non-hierarchical and non-judgemental. It is also grounded in the belief that everyone can improve and get better, and that everyone has something to offer to support this process, especially when co-coaching is used (i.e. A coaches B, then B coaches A). Everyone feels valued.

- As coaching develops across a school, more conversations take place about our core business – teaching and learning – and the school develops a coherent dialogue about pedagogy.

- Many CPD activities can be one-off events. At best, these result in a new strategy being tried out once or twice, but this improvement is rarely sustained and usually tails off. With coaching, because you know that you have committed to an undertaking and are going to be asked 'How's it been going?' when you next meet up with your coach, you are more likely to put it into action. If coaching meetings happen throughout the year, this improvement will be sustained.

- The one-size-fits-all approach to CPD (i.e. everyone sitting in a hall listening to the same message) is not an effective use of time. We all have our own personal areas of work that we want to develop, and coaching allows each of us to focus on what we want to improve. This is important if we want all teachers to be the best they possibly can be.

■ With coaching you choose the area you want to focus on – it is not dictated from above – so people feel empowered and motivated to improve.

Here are a few (real!) quotes from teachers who have tried out coaching:

The coach I worked with was really supportive. He helped me to work through the issue myself and find a solution. And it worked! As a result, I felt more confident to tackle issues on my own. Really good, thanks very much.

The best CPD I have had in the last three years. Brilliant.

I took the ideas on board that I discussed with my coach, used them with my classes and as a result felt more confident, organised and generally happier about how the first meetings with my new classes went. It has had a knock-on effect throughout the year with most of my classes.

Great to see the issue from another angle and come up with a solution – together.

Stay connected

■ Use the Twitter hashtag **#perfectcpdcoach** to share your experiences of coaching.

To-do list

- Decide on how you will use coaching:
  - A group of identified staff, prepared to coach their peers.
  - Staff who have a paid coaching role within the school.
  - Specialist coaching.
  - Whole-school coaching.
- Organise some coaching training for your coaches using the HILDA model.
- Consider how you will provide the time for the coaching to happen.
- Evaluate the impact of coaching and its contribution to teacher improvement.

Chapter 4

Learning Development Groups

Description

A learning development group (LDG) is a group of about twelve teachers (from different subject areas in secondary schools) who meet up on a regular basis throughout the school year to share best practice, support each other and commit to trying out new teaching strategies and/or resources. At the beginning of each session, each teacher describes and evaluates the new strategies or resources they have used since the last session.

> One of the most common characteristics of the survey schools was the effective work of one or more research and development groups. Their stated aim was to develop a whole-school policy or share good practice but they often achieved much more. In initiating what one leader called 'a continuous dialogue about learning', they increased staff's commitment to their own development and encouraged them to reflect on their own practice.
>
> Ofsted (2010: 17)

Each LDG has a specific pedagogical focus and teachers opt into the group that best suits their developmental priorities.

Implementation

There are four main stages to the implementation process.

1. Identify the focus of each LDG

The first stage is to identify the focus for each LDG that will run throughout the year. These will vary from school to school but should be clearly linked with the improvement priorities of the institution. For example, in my current school we had the following groups:

- Differentiation
- Literacy and communication

- Outstanding teaching
- The more able
- Assessment for Learning (AfL)
- Independent learning
- E-learning
- Effective middle leadership

An alternative approach is to have the same focus for each LDG, which is the methodology used with Teacher Learning Communities (TLCs), developed by Dylan Wiliam. TLCs consist of eight to ten classroom teachers who have decided to embed formative assessment techniques into their teaching. They meet regularly, report on their own progress and that of other TLC members based on short classroom observations, discuss ideas for improvement and agree what steps they will take before the next meeting.[1]

Once the themes for the LDGs have been decided they should be made available to the teaching staff. Teachers should then be asked to select, in consultation with their line manager and/or appraiser, which LDG they would like to join for that year. It is really important at this stage that teachers are encouraged to align their appraisal objectives with the LDG they are going to join. For example, if a teacher has said that they want to 'improve the progress made by the more able students they teach' as an appraisal objective, they should be encouraged to join the 'more able' LDG by their appraiser.

---

[1]   TLC resources are available to buy from <http://www.ssatuk.co.uk/ssat/support/teaching-and-learning/embedding-formative-assessment/>.

2. Identify LDG leaders

Once you have established the foci for each LDG, you will need to select a leader to run each session. They should have a keen interest in the area of pedagogy being developed in their group, be a good practitioner and be able to lead a session. Leading a workshop, such as a LDG, is in itself an excellent CPD opportunity for any aspiring school leader.

3. Allocate a time

Decide when the LDG sessions will run. For example, you could allocate a slot of 75–90 minutes on each INSET day for the LDGs to take place. It is helpful to schedule the LDGs during the early part of the day, so that when departments meet together later on, individuals can feed back on the LDG they have attended. This is an advantage of having 'themed' LDGs. It allows teachers from the same department to attend different LDGs and then share strategies when they come together as a team.

An alternative approach could be to 'disaggregate' an INSET day and use the time to run LDGs after school as discrete twilight sessions.

4. Running the sessions

LDG leaders will need to be briefed on how each session will run. For example:

- Each session should start with what progress has been made since the last meeting. Each person in the group describes and evaluates the new strategies/resources they have used since the last session.
- Input from the LDG leaders on new ideas and strategies to try out.
- Sharing of good practice as a group. What have they had success with? This can be done as a group or in pairs, which then feed back to the group.
- Everyone shares with the group what strategies they plan to develop, and how, in a plenary. They may also ask the group for ideas about how they can successfully implement the new strategy/resource.

During the session, teachers should be asked to complete a simple pro forma, summarising the session and their planned work after the session. This can then be added to the teacher's CPD file, as in the example overleaf.

1. Reflection on 'marginal learning gains' since the last LDG session ● What new strategies have you tried out since the last LDG sessions as a result of the discussions you had? ● What successes have you had? Why were they successful?	2. Summary of strategies discussed during your LDG session today	3. Action planning for more 'marginal learning gains' ● As a result of your discussions today, what new strategies are you going to try out and why – and with who? (link to appraisal objectives)

Case study: How Blatchington Mill School established Teacher Learning Communities

It seems obvious to state but professional development is a unique journey experience for every teacher. Too often, a production-line model of CPD has dominated in schools. Standardisation and homogeneity are valued over insight, innovation and ingenuity. Teaching has fundamental principles that underpin really excellent learning for all students, but the reality is that there are myriad ways in which to approach these tenets in the classroom. Put another way, I can't teach exactly the same way you can.

How many times have teachers gathered together at the start of a new term to be ushered into a whole-school lecture where a new technique, lesson-planning schema or pro forma is detailed that will be applied immediately to all lessons? How implausible it is that this concept will actually work to improve learning. Hobbes was right: we can be told something or we can understand how something works. CPD needs to be participant led, otherwise it is wasteful, ineffective and can detract from what is important in the classroom.

We have to consider the input–impact ratio with CPD: how much can we improve teaching in our classrooms by delivering more information in whole-staff briefings? We need to engage all teachers in their own self-reflection, and Teacher Learning Communities are part of the answer. Support networks where the local, the peer and the informal are valued developmental tools for improving your own practice only go so far. We cannot rely on peer support alone to improve our practice – nor should we. We need to mix the formal and the informal, the structured and the interpreted, the national and the local. And we need room within that to experiment, to find the better path or to fail gloriously.

At Blatch, we have tried to achieve this. Formal structures that place high value on teacher development – combined with personalised CPD, individual action research, and a mixture of internal and external expertise. Every teacher needs to be catered for individually within a secure system that gives credit for the process of self-development as well as the outcomes. Every teacher, whether they are flying or falling, should be challenged and supported to get better.

The first stage is to identify what is central about learning that should be sought in all lessons. That sounds straightforward but half an hour on Twitter will reveal just how much dispute exists! At Blatch, we start with Ron Berger's *An Ethic of Excellence* (2003) for student outcomes: expect excellent outcomes and products of learning. We then have a short set of principles for lesson design. In brief, start the core learning as quickly as possible, make the purpose of the lesson explicit, use AfL, make it engaging to get students involved and use short feedback loops to test understanding. Beyond these principles, we then work as a whole staff to investigate the most effective ways of delivering on these objectives. Every single teacher completes an action research project tied to our development plan for teaching and learning. These are supported by lead professionals who act as guides, mentors and coaches for those in their TLC.

Each TLC has a specific focus (there were eight in 2013/2014) and these foci connect together to ensure that the aspects of our teaching that we want to examine and improve are covered by us all as a team. The foci come from extensive and ongoing analysis of lesson observations across the school, as well as what the data tells us we should focus on to improve teaching. They also reflect our strengths. Where the same data sets suggest we are performing well, we explore what has created success and spread what worked. Staff can move between foci as their needs and interests develop. Started looking to shorten feedback loops for students in September but now have it cracked and want to look at SOLO learning intentions? Not a problem. The breadth of the programme means that teachers can progress faster than we ever could as a 'herd' in whole-staff, straightjacketed CPD programmes.

One teacher can't investigate in depth and detail 110 separate areas of teaching practice every year, but if we coordinate as a school we can. We build in meeting time over the year to reflect on the progress we are making with each project, adapt them, extend them and share them as a staff. The lead professionals are the master strategists who keep each project moving forwards.

On top of this, we layer optional teaching and learning workshops throughout the year. These are generated from staff requests, school priorities, identified needs or national developments. They hinge around the *Teachers' Standards* – ensuring all staff are supported in meeting them.

Finally, be brave about failure. As long as every objective is set out with a valid enquiry, avoiding known pitfalls and educational myths, then failure is as important to the individual and the institution as a successful outcome. So, you set out to improve learning for Pupil Premium students by using technology to enhance home-school communication but there is negligible impact on performance in the classroom. What happens then? Shrug and move on? No, we dig deeper. Share in failures as a staff and examine what would happen differently if we tweaked the approach. Is it workable in a different way? Does it expose a deeper flaw? Does it tell you something about yourself as a teacher? If you are serious about achieving excellence, you agonise over the details – and that means allowing CPD to expose failure *and* success. Students and teachers deserve no less.

Ashley Harrold, **@BMS_MrHarrold**, deputy head teacher, Blatchington Mill School, Hove, East Sussex

Evaluation

Learning development groups offer numerous benefits as a CPD strategy:

- As each LDG has a particular 'theme' it allows teachers to align their CPD with their own improvement priorities.
- The fact that the themes for the different LDGs can be directly aligned to whole-school improvement priorities makes it a very focused form of CPD.
- Leading a LDG is great CPD for aspiring leaders.
- At the start of every session, everyone has to discuss the new strategies/resources they have tried out since the last session. As this is quite public, they are more likely to have tried something.
- LDGs are another opportunity for teachers to share best practice.
- The sessions can act as a catalyst for future collaborative work (e.g. joint planning, peer observation, co-coaching).

- In secondary schools there are few opportunities for staff from different subjects to work together. LDGs provide the opportunity to do this.

- LDG leaders need to ensure that they include everybody in the discussions and don't allow people to sit back passively.

- LDGs provide an opportunity for celebrating success at the end of the school year. For example, each group could present their most successful strategies/resources to the rest of the staff. Alternatively a 'marketplace' event could be held: two or three people from each LDG host a 'stall' in the school hall, where they display and discuss resources and strategies from their LDG.

Stay connected

- Use the Twitter hashtag **#perfectcpdldg** to share your experiences of working in a learning development group.

To-do list

- Decide on a theme for your LDGs which should ✓
  be aligned to your whole-school development
  targets.
- Allocate time for the LDG sessions to happen ✓
  (e.g. during INSET days or staff meetings).
- Identify your LDG leaders. ✓
- Familiarise the LDG leaders with the resources ✓
  and format of the sessions.
- Put staff into LDGs – decide if these will be ✓
  cross-curricular or within subject teams.

- Ensure there is a way of staff recording what ✓
  strategies they plan to implement as a result of
  the LDG, so that this can be referred to and
  reviewed at the next session.

Chapter 5

Action Research

Description

There is much discussion in the world of education about educational research. What it is? What it isn't? What's good about it? What's bad about it?

The most important aspect of research is that teachers are allowed to follow their own pedagogical interests, find out what works and then share it. For some teachers, this may involve following a Master's-level programme in education. Alternatively, you may wish to adopt a more classroom-based approach.

In my school, teachers can apply for a 'learning innovator' role. Successful applicants carry out a one-year action research project on an area of pedagogy that interests them and which also aligns with the improvement priorities of the school. Once the project is completed at the end of the year, they receive a small payment for their work.

Implementation

If you decide to go down the learning innovator role route, staff first need to be invited to submit an application for the post. For example, you could send a letter to all staff giving clear guidance about the application process:

Dear _____,

This academic year will be the third year of our successful, personalised CPD programme. It is an opportunity for teaching staff to carry out an enquiry-based, best-practice project over the course of a year, on an area of pedagogy that interests them and also links to the improvement priorities of the school.

For this year, we are particularly interested in proposals that focus on developing innovative approaches to the following areas:

E-learning

Literacy

Questioning

Feedback

Independence

Challenging the more able

Last year we were able to fund four action research projects, carried out by _____. They will be happy to discuss their projects with you, if you require further information.

Your project should have an impact on not only your own practice but also that of other staff, both within and outside of your department.

You will be expected to attend fortnightly meetings to discuss your work, prepare a written report on your findings once you have completed your research and then share these with the staff.

A payment of £500 will be available. This will be paid upon completion of the project.

Places will be limited, so if there is a lot of interest in this opportunity a selection process might be required.

If this is something you are interested in, you will need to submit a project proposal (no more than two sides of A4), expressing:

- The area you would like to focus on and how this fits in with the improvement priorities of your department and the school.
- An outline plan of how you intend to carry out your project.
- Why you think this will be important to the continued improvement of the school.

> ■ How the impact of your project will be widened beyond your own practice.
>
> ■ How you will measure the impact of your work.

Depending on the level of interest (and the number of posts you are able to fund) you might need to interview applicants. Here are some examples of action research projects that teachers have undertaken:

■ Developing teaching strategies and activities based on Key Stage 1 and 2 pedagogy to improve engagement and differentiation in maths lessons.

■ Using SOLO taxonomy to provide a structured learning and thinking framework, and thereby developing students as active participants in the learning process.

■ What AfL teaching strategies really make a difference to student learning?

■ How can 'flipped learning' be used effectively to deepen learning?

■ How can we develop independence in students, and what is the impact of this on learning?

Once you have selected your group of learning innovators, or whatever you choose to call them, the format of the project needs to be agreed. The following set-up has delivered successful outcomes in many schools:

Term 1

- Initial research into the area of pedagogy you are focusing on (e.g. school(s), literature, internet).
- Development of own practice. Use your initial research to develop your own classroom practice.
- How will you know that the project has had an impact?

Term 2

- Development and consolidation of own practice.
- Widening involvement across the department. Encourage and support other members of your department to implement these strategies/resources.

Term 3

- Development and consolidation across the department.
- Widening involvement to other subjects. How can the strategies/resources you have developed be transferred to other curriculum areas?
- What has been the impact of your project?
- Future developments.

At the beginning of the project, it is helpful if the researchers produce a work plan to assist them in focusing their work. Here is an exemplar work plan for an action research project.

Action research work plan

Name:

Title:

Objectives:

Give a brief outline of what you hope to achieve with this project.

How will you know if you have been successful?

What impact measures will you use to judge whether or not your work has been successful? Include milestones for these measures and how you will establish a baseline to measure from.

Plan

Term 1:

- Initial research (e.g. school(s), literature, internet).
- Development of own practice.
- Measuring impact.

Time	Actions (bullet point)	By who	Desired outcomes

Review and evaluation of Term 1 work

Term 2:

- Development and consolidation of own practice.
- Widening involvement across the department.

Time	Actions (bullet point)	By who	Desired outcomes

Review and evaluation of Term 2 work

Term 3:

- Development and consolidation across the department.
- Widening involvement to other subjects.

- Impact of project.
- Future developments.

Time	Actions (bullet point)	By who	Desired outcomes

At the end of Term 3, a full report will be written on the project and a brief summary presented to the whole staff.

A work plan helps to give the project a formal structure and ensures there is progression throughout the year; that is, it moves from personal development to working with departmental colleagues and then to colleagues outside of your subject area.

Fortnightly meetings with a project coordinator (such as the school CPD coordinator) are also a very important feature of action research projects. These help to keep the project on track, while also providing an opportunity for the researchers to bounce ideas around.

When staff commit time and effort into researching and developing good practice in this way, it is very important that it is shared with the whole staff. This can be done by committing a staff meeting at the end of the year to presentations by your researchers about their projects. This can be both useful and uplifting in terms of sharing great ideas. Too little time is spent in schools celebrating the excellent work of our staff, so opportunities like this should be fully exploited. In his book, *An Ethic of Excellence*, Ron Berger describes his experience of spending time with teachers who are engaged in action research:

> In the past 10 years I've had the privilege of spending time with many teachers who are investigating their practice. The excitement and knowledge that they develop is universal. Just like with students, the pressure that comes with making their work public compels them to put unusual effort and thoughtfulness into their practice.
>
> Berger (2003: 131)

Evaluation

These reflections from past learning innovators at Durrington High School give a good flavour of some of the personal benefits of carrying out an action research project:

> I would encourage all teachers to undertake research projects as part of their professional development. My experience was really positive. It made me more confident, it made me think about the way I taught and the way students learn.
>
> Simona Trignano (2013)

> Throughout the project I have also had the opportunity to discuss what I have been doing with other members of the department and wider staff body through a 15 minute forum. I have had CPD sessions with teachers from drama and English, where they have already begun to embed ICT and the use of iPads into their teaching. I have also been able to share my ideas and findings with the wider teaching community through writing a blog which was shared on social networking sites and put on various PE websites.
>
> I believe that this learning innovator project will serve as an excellent foundation for future development and the integration of ICT into our whole school community.
>
> Lizzie Wolstenholme (2013)

> This research project has developed my understanding
> of differentiation. I have researched the different strate-
> gies and I have been able to observe how these strategies
> are implemented to create high quality learning experi-
> ences for pupils. I have equipped myself with new
> differentiation strategies which I have used to improve
> my own teaching. I have also been able to share ideas
> within my school community.
>
> Rachael Strong (2012)

Research and development should be a key focus for all
schools if we are serious about developing high quality and
innovative approaches to teaching in our institutions.

- It allows staff to follow their own pedagogical interests.
- By enabling action research you are developing 'experts'
  in a particular field within your institution, who can
  then go on to support others.
- It is a great way of developing an outward-looking
  approach and bringing in new ideas from other schools
  and institutions.
- It is a great way of retaining recently qualified teachers
  (RQTs).
- It is a very good way of building leadership capacity
  within a school, as the projects require colleagues to
  work with a wide range of different people. (I know of a
  number of colleagues who have completed an action

research project and then gone on to secure a leadership promotion.)

▨ It ensures school improvement priorities retain a high profile.

▨ It encourages collaboration and a dialogue about pedagogy within the school.

Stay connected

▨ Read the learning innovator reports from Durrington High School at http://classteaching.wordpress.com/.

▨ Use the Twitter hashtag **#perfectedcpdresearch** to share your experiences of educational action research.

To-do list

▨ Decide (a) how much you will pay staff who engage with action research, (b) if there are any preferred foci for your action research projects and (c) how many projects you are willing to fund. ☑

▨ Offer the opportunity for action research to your staff. ☑

▨ Decide whose projects you will fund from all the proposals received. ☑

- Start the projects by discussing the research question in detail and agreeing how the project will develop each term.
- Plan regular review meetings. ☑

Chapter 6

Professional Learning Visits

Description

When teachers are given the opportunity to visit another school, they often return with comments along the lines of 'that was the best CPD I've had for a long while'. This is not surprising. It is very easy for schools to get 'stuck' in terms of how they do things, so when an issue arises it is difficult to consider alternative solutions. Visiting another school often allows us to see different approaches to common problems and gives us a fresh perspective on our own school.

Therefore, it is unfortunate that there are usually very few opportunities for teachers to go on learning visits. Alongside issues such as the cost of cover when staff are absent on a school visit, there is also the problem of finding schools that are suitable and willing to host a visit.

However, these obstacles can be overcome. For example, using an INSET day to send everybody out to another school to find good practice and bring inspiration back to the school is a powerful way to gain new perspectives and ideas. In his book, *High Performers*, Alistair Smith looks at what successful schools do. He has found that a key aspect of their success is being outward looking:

> Scan the horizon to understand what's possible. Get out of school to see the best of what's around. Collaborate like mad; share like it's only just been invented! Once you find a great organisation, website, network, school department or pioneer, then stay close.
>
> Smith (2011: 171)

Implementation

The idea of using an INSET day to send everyone on a visit to another school sounds like a very simple one. The practicalities are far from straightforward though. Leave yourself plenty of time to get it organised – at least 12 months!

The first stage is to establish which schools would be willing to host a visit. This is best done by sending a letter to the surrounding schools and asking if they would be willing to host a professional learning visit. A sample letter might read as follows:

Dear Head Teacher,

I am currently in the process of planning the CPD programme for _____ School for next year. The underlying theme for our programme is sharing best practice through effective collaboration within our school, but also with other schools. I believe that we have a huge amount to learn from each other.

With this in mind, a key part of our CPD programme for next year will be professional learning visits. On [date], we are planning to send all of our teaching staff to visit another school to see best practice in an area of their choice. In order to facilitate this, it would be really useful to know if you would be willing to accommodate a visit from a member of our teaching staff to your school on this day.

Please could you complete the attached form and send it back to me by [date]. This gives you the opportunity to express in which areas you would be willing to host a professional learning visit. I can then use this when planning the arrangements. Hopefully these visits will start up a dialogue between colleagues and lead to further collaborative work, which would benefit both schools involved.

Once we have collated all of the good practice from these visits into a project document, a copy will be sent to all the schools that supported the project. Schools will also be invited to any project dissemination events based here at _____ School.

I would like to express my sincere thanks for your support with this project. If you have any questions about the visits, please feel free to contact me.

Yours sincerely,

Here is a sample form for schools to complete and return to you:

Professional learning visits

School name/address ....

Contact name ....

Role ....

Email ....

We would/would not be willing to host a professional learning visit on [date].

We are happy to accommodate staff in the following areas (please indicate how many staff you could accommodate in each area):

Subject area	Maximum no. of staff for visit
English	
Maths	
Science	
ICT	
Art	
Business studies	
Drama	
Design and technology	
Geography	
History	
Media	
MFL	
Music	
PE	

Whole school	Maximum no. of staff for visit
General	
E-learning	
Student well-being/pastoral care	
Use of data	
Behaviour management	
Curriculum	
Alternative curriculum provision	
Improving teaching and learning	
Student voice	
More able	
Transition	
Other – please add:	

As schools reply, and with any luck offer to host a visit, you can begin to build up a database of schools and the focus of the visits they are willing to accommodate. On the whole, schools are keen to get involved with this type of collaborative working and so are usually very generous with their time.

The next stage is to find out what your staff would like as the focus of their professional learning visit. Use an exemplar planning form like the one below to canvass their views.

Professional learning visit

What will be the focus of your visit?

How does this link to your appraisal objectives?

PLEASE TICK ONE OF THE BOXES BELOW

I have arranged the following visit for myself: ☐

School/establishment ....

Name of contact ....

I would like the visit arranged for me. ☐

Your teachers will have a number of contacts in other schools, so they may well be able (and willing) to arrange their own visit. It is important to stress that they should think very carefully about what they want to get from the visit and how this fits in with their own personal development, which should have been highlighted during the appraisal process (see Chapter 1 for more on this).

You will now have all of the information you need to assign a host school to each member of staff. This can then be confirmed with a letter to each participating school.

Dear Head Teacher,

Thank you for contacting me to confirm that your school would be willing to support us with our CPD programme this year. As you know, the underlying theme for this programme is sharing best practice through effective collaboration within our school, but also with other schools, through professional learning visits.

On [date], we are planning to send all of our teaching staff out to visit another school to see best practice in an area of their choice. We are now in a position to allocate staff to schools. As a school that has very kindly agreed to take part in this programme, we would like to ask you to host the following members of our staff on [date]:

Staff name	Role	Area to visit

Please could you confirm that you are happy for these visits to take place using the slip below. Staff will arrive with you by 8.30 a.m. on the day of the visit.

I would like to express my sincere thanks for your support with this project. If you have any questions about the visits, please feel free to contact me.

Yours sincerely,

Once the visits have taken place, staff should then review their visit. They will need to be given appropriate documentation, such as an exemplar learning pro forma like the one below, ahead of the visit so they know what they should be looking for during the day.

Professional learning visit review

Name ....

School visited ....

Please use the spaces below to identify any good practice that you picked up during your visit in the following areas. (Please indicate with a * any you will implement immediately.)

Teaching and learning (including e-learning and the use of innovative technology)

Department-based (e.g. scheme of work, curriculum, enrichment, assessment)

Pastoral and well-being (ideas that could support the children's progress and well-being)

Specific to any leadership responsibility you may have

Whole-school (e.g. curriculum, reports, assessment, data and monitoring, behaviour, CPD, rewards, student voice, literacy, independent learning, efficient working practice)

Actions as a result of the visit:

- What will you be putting into place regarding your own practice?
- How will you share any departmental strategies?
- Who do you plan to share any other strategies with and how?

Once the visits have taken place, there are a number of ways in which you can disseminate and/or develop the information:

- Collate the ideas into a booklet or website.
- Staff presentations during INSET days.
- Ask everyone to contribute at least three ideas they have gathered into their own 'department improvement plan' or any other improvement plan.
- A 'good ideas board' in the staffroom.

An alternative approach to sending everybody out on the same day is to issue all members of staff with a one-day personal learning visit voucher for the year. In terms of organisation, this is far simpler to implement.

Personal Learning Voucher

This voucher (when presented to the cover department) entitles the named person below to one day of cover to visit another school and find some good ideas:

Name: ....

Date of visit: ....

School visiting: ....

Conditions:

1. Agreement by the cover manager is dependent on the cover demands that day.

2. The teacher must complete a personal learning visit feedback form following the visit.

Chapter 6

Evaluation

Professional learning visits are a great CPD strategy that can potentially capture a huge amount of good practice. In order to be successful, it is worth considering the following points:

- It is important to get teachers to think carefully beforehand about what the focus of their visit will be.
- Consider when the visits should take place. If it is too late in the summer term, much of the momentum can be lost during the summer break.
- Consider how the information you gather will be disseminated, put into action and then monitored.

Stay connected

- Use the Twitter hashtag **#perfectcpdplv** if you are interested in visiting another school to share best practice or to share good ideas you have gleaned from visiting another school.

To-do list

- ☑ Decide on a date for your professional learning visit.

- ☑ Contact local schools to see if they would be interested in hosting learning visits.

- ☑ Ask all teachers if they will be arranging their own learning visit or if they want you to arrange it for them.

- ☑ Ask all teachers what they want the focus of their learning visit to be.

- ☑ Match teachers to a suitable school.

- ☑ Communicate the details of each professional learning visit to teachers and the school that will be visited.

- ☑ Before the visit, make sure staff are clear about what you want them to get out of the visit.

- ☑ After the visit, think about how you will collate and distribute the ideas.

Chapter 7
INSET Days and Staff Meetings

Description

INSET days and staff meetings probably don't take much describing! They are what they are and schools will use them in a variety of ways to best suit their needs and priorities. However, having the whole teaching staff in a room together is a CPD opportunity that should be exploited – an opportunity to share and discuss what works well in a time-efficient way. What follows are some simple strategies that can be implemented to achieve this.

Implementation

Here are seven simple strategies to achieve some CPD during meetings and INSET days.

1. Marginal learning gains board

Before each staff meeting, place small cards (like the one below) on each chair.

Teaching tweak

Marginal learning gain

While staff are waiting for the meeting to start, they should write down one small change they have made to an aspect of their teaching – a 'teaching tweak'. This might be a new teaching strategy or resource. They should then write down the 'marginal learning gain' from this – what difference the tweak makes to student learning. At the end of the meeting, the cards can be collected in and displayed somewhere prominent for all to see.

2. Big idea booklets

Big idea booklets are an extension of the marginal learning gains board. If, as a school, you are looking to develop a specific aspect of pedagogy, put a 'big idea' sheet on each chair or table at the start of a staff meeting. Ask teachers to share one good strategy they have used. The example below focuses on questioning.

The BIG idea

The effective use of questioning is an essential aspect of quality teaching. In terms of planning questions to assess key learning this means: when they are asked, how they are asked, what prompts are used to support questioning, ensuring all students are involved, ensuring that questioning is scaffolded to develop student responses, ensuring that questioning is challenging, providing opportunities for students to come up with their own questions, etc.

In order to share successful strategies we have used to develop effective questioning, can you take a minute or two to jot down one method you have used to do this in the space below – no matter how simple it seems.

I will then collate them and distribute.

Name:
Successful method I have used to develop questioning:

Please leave this on your seat.

These sheets can then be collated into a booklet and distributed to all teaching staff. Below is an example of effective techniques to check learning.

Successful methods used to check learning:

Review of work mid-lesson, looking at GCSE assessment criteria.

Getting students to identify what they need to do to move forward.

Use of sticky notes.

Red, amber, green cards to check understanding of technique/process.

Steve Bloomer – Art and Design

Red, amber, green cards in back of planner – when introducing new words/tools/processes in lesson students are to leave planners open according to how confident they are with explaining/using/recalling word. Teacher can then recap as appropriate before end of lesson.

Emma Wade – Design and Technology

The free programme 'Socrative', this programme allows you to use exit tickets, surveys, quizzes.

I also like to use presentations and letting students teach other students showing that they have learned it while teaching other students.

Chris Mellett – Business and ICT

'Spotlight' – without prior warning, asking a student to stand up and describe what they are doing, why they are doing it and how they are doing it (usually used when students are working in groups).

David Hall – Drama

Letters on planners
Mini whiteboards
Stand up/sit down
Throw the dolphin
Green, amber, red cards in planners out on desks
Post it notes
5 - 4 - 3 - 2 - 1 punch the wall

Simona Trigano – Science

3. Mini TeachMeet

TeachMeets will be discussed in more detail in Chapter 9. While these usually consist of teachers from a number of schools gathering together to share best practice, they can also be done on a smaller scale.

Schools could put aside a staff meeting, or a slot during an INSET day, for staff to do a 'micro-presentation' (7 minutes) on a teaching strategy or resource that they have been using or developing. As each presentation is very short, you can get through a good number in a short period of time.

4. Whole-school 15 minute forum

The 15 minute forum was discussed in Chapter 2, where we learned that they are a brilliant way to share best practice throughout the school. However, as they tend to be optional, staff who have yet to attend one may not be aware of how useful they can be. The staff meeting provides a captive audience to showcase the merit of the 15 minute forum.

Start a staff meeting or INSET day with a member of staff leading a 15 minute forum for the whole staff. Not only will this allow you to share a successful strategy or two but it will also show staff how useful 15 minute forums are – hopefully boosting attendance at other forums.

5. Speed pedagogy sharing

Speed pedagogy sharing is based on the principle of speed dating! Half of the teaching staff (group A) sit at separate desks and the other half (group B) choose to sit with someone from group A. They then have five minutes to share a successful strategy with each other. A bell then sounds, everyone moves round one place and the process is repeated. Each person can be scored for how good their strategy is, with the most successful ones being shared.

6. Pedagogy marketplace

Each department sets up a 'stall' in a large open place, such as the hall, where they showcase some of their best teaching strategies and resources. Staff can then wander round, pick up great ideas from other departments and discuss how they could be transferred to their department. By organising the stalls by department, teachers can take it in turns to 'staff' the stall, giving everyone the opportunity to browse what's on offer. This could be extended to include other schools, to encourage greater collaborative working between schools.

7. Modelling lessons

The simple idea of one teacher modelling a particular teaching strategy to their peers can be organised in a variety of ways:

- Live lesson – a 'temporary classroom' is set up in the middle of a large space (i.e. with chairs, tables, board, projector, etc.). The teacher then teaches a lesson to a group of students. Meanwhile, other teachers observe the lesson from the sides of the room.

- Teaching the teachers – teachers are organised into 'classes' which then attend a lesson taught by a teacher who is modelling a particular strategy. This is usually best done during an INSET day, when each 'class' of teachers can rotate round a number of different lessons and be taught by different teachers. Each teacher could focus on the same teaching strategy but from a different perspective or each teacher could focus on a different strategy.

■ Video lesson – a teacher could record themselves modelling a particular teaching strategy. The rest of the teaching staff could then watch the video, with the teacher giving a running commentary and taking questions.

Evaluation

There are always lots of exciting and innovative activities going on in classrooms. As school leaders, we need to be hunting them out and sharing them across the school. Strategies like the ones discussed in this chapter provide schools with simple and time-efficient ways to do just this.

Stay connected

■ Use the Twitter hashtag **#perfectcpdinset** to share your successes with these strategies or any similar strategies with which you've had success.

To-do list

- Decide on which strategy you are going to use for each INSET day. ☑

- Ensure any participating staff are fully briefed before the day. ☑

- Make it very clear what you want staff to get out of the session. ☑

- Ensure you plan in a summary at the end of the session and an opportunity later in the year to reflect on the impact of the session. ☑

Chapter 8

Lesson Observation Review and Reflection

Description

The '5 minute lesson review' was produced by me and Ross McGill (**@TeacherToolkit**). It supports and encourages teachers to reflect on their own classroom practice following a lesson observation. Lesson observations should be a formative process for teachers during which they are encouraged to evaluate and develop their practice. They should not be just about being given a grade for the quality of teaching. In his book, *Visible Learning*, John Hattie discusses the importance of teacher reflection:

> [T]he act of teaching reaches its epitome of success after the lesson has been structured, after the content has been delivered, and after the classroom has been organised. The art of teaching, and its major successes, relate to 'what happens next'.
>
> Hattie (2009: 1–2)

The 5 minute review template can also be used by a coach or mentor to help tease out reflection. As professionals, we all want to be the best we can be. But in order to do so, we need to be encouraged and supported to reflect on our own classroom practice in a focused and time-efficient way. We then need to commit to action. The 5 minute lesson review supports this process.

This type of reflection and review can also be enhanced by the use of video observation technology.

Implementation

A diagram of the 5 minute lesson review appears below. Following a lesson observation, the observer should give a copy to the observed teacher, who should go away, reflect on the lesson and complete the review. When the observer and teacher meet for the lesson debrief, the review will form the basis for their discussion.

Below is a breakdown of how to complete each stage of the review process.

My personal targets

The targets section is for the teacher to note down what aspect of their teaching they are looking to develop in the lesson. This may have come out of a mentoring meeting for an NQT, an appraisal meeting for a more experienced mem-

The 5 Minute Lesson Review
Produced by **@shaun_allison** and **@TeacherToolkit**

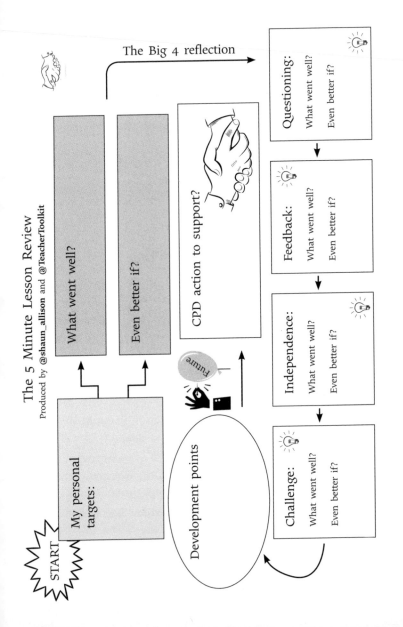

ber of staff, a coaching meeting between two teachers or just an area that the teacher wants to develop. For example:

- Behaviour management of small groups of boys (name the specific students whose behaviour you are looking to address).
- Making sure my questioning involves a wide number of students and develops 'deep thinking'.
- Ensuring that the more able students within the class are stretched and challenged.

What went well?/Even better if?

WWW and EBI represent the first stage of the reflection process following the observed lesson. The teacher should think about the personal targets they set for themselves for the lesson and then consider the success they had with it and how it could have been further improved. For example:

WWW – boys were focused and on-task at the start of the lesson due to the engaging hook.

EBI – this focus wasn't then lost during the written activity when they had to work independently.

WWW – using lolly sticks ensured that more students were more involved in the questioning. Not knowing if they were going to be asked also kept them focused.

EBI – I asked more questions, based on their responses, to further develop their thinking.

The Big 4 reflection

Having reflected on their personal targets, the teacher is now encouraged to reflect on four key aspects of pedagogical excellence – questioning, feedback, independence and challenge – which are also fundamental for outstanding teaching. For each of the four reflections, the teacher is encouraged to evaluate what went well for each aspect and what they need to develop further.

There is no reason why different schools couldn't adjust 'The Big 4' to fit with their own specific improvement priorities.

Development points

Having now reflected on their personal targets and 'The Big 4', the teacher should now come up with one or two overall development points that they want to address in their teaching – based on the EBIs from the earlier section. By identifying just one or two aspects to develop, the process of self-improvement is kept realistic, manageable and specific.

CPD action to support

Having identified some specific development points to address, the teacher now needs to consider what CPD they will undertake to support this improvement. For example:

- Peer observation
- Coaching

- Collaborative planning
- Attend a school CPD discussion
- Video lesson
- Action research project
- Blog review
- Trial lesson again with similar key stage/class
- Lesson study

If they are working with a facilitator (e.g. coach, appraiser), it is important that the facilitator encourages and teases the solutions out of the teacher, rather than providing them themselves. This will hopefully lead to deeper and more frequent self-realisation and reflection in the future.

Video observation technology

A recent development in lesson observations has been the advancement of video technology from companies such as IRIS Connect. This form of web-based technology means that a mobile camera set up in a classroom can be controlled remotely by a PC, with facilities such as full rotation of the lens, high-quality zoom and sound recording.

Video observation technology is a very powerful CPD and reflection tool for teachers and can be used in a variety of ways:

- A teacher records a lesson (or segment of a lesson – you decide) and then watches it back. They can choose to watch it on their own, as a self-reflection exercise, or with a colleague.

- Real-time coaching. A colleague observes a lesson remotely and coaches the teacher being observed during the lesson using a microphone link-up. This is particularly useful if the teacher wants to focus on a specific aspect of their teaching (e.g. referring back to the learning objectives).

- A teacher can choose an area of teaching they want to develop, then carry out a paired remote observation with another teacher who demonstrates good practice in this area.

The central idea with this technology is that the teacher controls how it is used and for what purpose.

Case study: What the academic research says about video observation technology

Dr Brian Marsh (**@brianmarsh52**) from the School of Education at the University of Brighton has been undertaking academic research on video observation technology in classrooms for a number of years. He sees the benefits of this technology as:

- Capturing data which reflects and preserves the complexity of observed activities.

- Accessing detailed descriptions of classroom dynamics that are hard or impossible to access or describe in other ways.

- Allowing viewers to follow the unfolding of complex social events over time, such as watching how teachers employ particular strategies to deal with diverse classroom situations.

His research suggests that the critical viewing of videoed lessons is beneficial in developing general pedagogical content knowledge, subject knowledge and subject pedagogical knowledge. This is because:

- Critical mediated viewing allows for a meaningful understanding of what is viewed, often deconstructed into constituent parts and sometimes reconstructed to get a holistic view.

- It enhances teachers' powers of reflection and analysis (at whatever stage of their career) and generates deeper reflection about what they would do next time (e.g. Why did I do that? What learning occurred?). This form of reflection leads to constructive changes to practice.

- It opens up the language of pedagogy, which is particularly important early in a teacher's career. Discussing teaching methodology can be a powerful learning tool.

■ It facilitates collaborative learning, meaning that teachers become learners.

Over a series of four videoed observations of one teacher, the following changes were noted in terms of their reflections about the lesson:

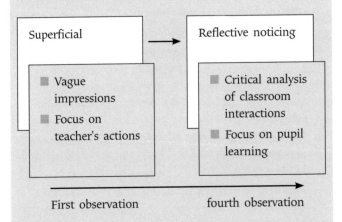

Superficial → Reflective noticing

■ Vague impressions
■ Focus on teacher's actions

■ Critical analysis of classroom interactions
■ Focus on pupil learning

First observation → fourth observation

Dr Marsh suggests that the following issues should be considered by schools when introducing video observation technology:

■ Lesson observation can be difficult for early-career teachers as they may not know what they are looking for, so they should be given plenty of guidance.

- More experienced teachers may find it hard to avoid viewing video observations through the lens of their background experience. This has the potential to limit their learning, so they should be supported to avoid this problem.

- The skill of 'noticing' (i.e. identifying what is relevant) needs to be developed with staff. They should be encouraged to be focused and selective.

- Observations should have a distinct focus (e.g. How are transition points managed between episodes in lessons? How is formative assessment undertaken? Is questioning open or closed? How is differentiation achieved?).

- Evidence suggests that observations are ineffective if undertaken alone, so peer-based review is crucial in supporting professional learning. The use of a mentor or coach is critical, but only if an approach along these lines is used:

1. The lesson is recorded.

2. Both teacher and coach view it alone.

3. They come together to discuss the lesson.

4. Agreed targets are set for development.

5. The lesson is repeated after an agreed period of time.

6. Teacher and coach go through the process for several cycles.

This approach can be further developed by using a 'supportive professional development group'. With this method, a lesson is recorded of each group member, followed by a group discussion of that lesson. This is repeated with all members of the group. The process is then repeated with group-determined targets.

There is no evidence that subject-based groups are more or less effective than cross-curricular groups, although a key feature is quality feedback from trusted, critical friends. This approach has the added benefit of shaping the professional development of a group of colleagues.

In addition to Dr Marsh's advice, schools should answer the following questions before rolling out video observations:

- Who will have ownership of the video? (Ideally it should belong to the teacher being videoed.)
- Will teachers have the option of using video technology or will they be obliged to use it?
- What happens if the lesson dies? If possible, the teacher should have the right for it not to be seen, although most do because there is, of course, learning in failure.
- Should videoed observations be used for appraisal? Evidence suggests that the technology is most effective when it is kept separate from assessment, but that will be for individual schools to decide.

▓ Students need to be considered too, so ensure you have permission from parents/guardians. If video observation is used regularly then students will soon get used to it and ignore the camera.

Evaluation

The 5 minute lesson review works because:

▓ The teacher has ownership over their own personal development.

▓ Analysing practice supports teachers' self-reflection.

▓ Reviewing practice ensures that CPD is targeted towards teachers' own developmental targets.

▓ Reflecting on practice focuses teachers on the key features of good/outstanding teaching – questioning, feedback, independence and challenge.

▓ Appraising practice encourages teachers to think carefully about just one or two improvement priorities, which keeps the review manageable and realistic.

▓ Recapping on practice makes appraisal objectives more 'live' and relevant.

▓ Critiquing practice encourages teachers to commit to action.

▓ Reflecting on practice can support the coaching process by acting as a starting point for a coaching conversation.

Stay connected

- Download a copy of the 5 minute lesson review from http://classteaching.wordpress.com/.
- Use the Twitter hashtag **#5minreview** to share your experiences of using the 5 minute lesson review and to post photos of completed examples.

To-do list

- Consider how the 5 minute lesson review will be used across the school (e.g. Do you expect it to be used for all lesson observations or will it be optional?). ✓
- Take the time to do some training with teachers about how it can be used – go through each stage carefully. ✓
- Share examples of good practice with the teaching staff. ✓
- Introduce video observation technology to the teaching staff as a developmental and reflective tool. ✓
- Encourage some 'keen' teachers to use the video observation and share their experiences with their peers. ✓
- Offer the opportunity of a video observation to all staff via email or flyers. ✓

Chapter 9

TeachMeets

Description

TeachMeets – which are free, informal conferences for teachers, by teachers – are becoming more commonplace across the country. Each TeachMeet consists of a programme of micro-presentations, each one no longer than seven minutes. These micro-presentations may be about a teaching strategy, a specific resource or both. TeachMeets are about hearing real stories about learning from real teachers, based on successes they have had in their own classrooms. These are often powerful narratives of practice that make a genuine difference to student learning.

Implementation

Staging a TeachMeet can be a highly rewarding experience. The following points should hopefully make the event easier to organise.

1. Decide on a focus

Most TeachMeets have a general focus and teachers are free to talk about any aspect of pedagogy they choose. There are some alternatives though:

▓ LeadMeets – instead of focusing on pedagogy, school leaders talk about aspects of their leadership work that have made a difference in their schools.

▓ Subject-specific – a TeachMeet aimed at specific curriculum areas (e.g. science, English).

▓ Research-based – many teachers are becoming more interested in developing an evidence-based approach to teacher development. The TeachMeet format provides schools and universities with an opportunity to work collaboratively to share educational research.

2. Set up a wiki for your event

There is a national wiki site where you can promote your event: http://teachmeet.pbworks.com/. Once you have registered and published your event details, people can use the site to sign up to attend the event, either as a presenter or just to come along.

3. Recruit your presenters

The quality of the presenters is what makes a successful TeachMeet, so use your network of teachers within and beyond your school to encourage them to deliver a presentation. This may include teachers within your own school who have led CPD sessions, great classroom practitioners who have developed interesting or innovative approaches to teaching, or teachers who are engaged with action research. In terms of reaching out beyond your school, Twitter is a great way of finding presenters from elsewhere, or try sending an email to neighbouring schools.

It is essential to get a good balance of presentations at a TeachMeet, so it is worth mentioning to presenters that the event will be attended by teachers from all phases of education. With this in mind, they should try to plan their talk or demonstration so that the strategies and/or principles discussed are relevant to teachers from all phases. To give you an idea of the range, here is the list of presentations from the Durrington High School TeachMeet in 2013:

- Josie Maitland, The Angmering School – Inspire: Engaging Challenging Students
- Lianne Allison, The Angmering School – Developing Independence by Avoiding the Pitfalls of Praise (**@lianne_allison**)
- Matthew Fairbairn, Durrington High School – Computer-Based Problem Solving
- Lucy Darling, Durrington High School – Developing Questioning and P4C (**@DarlingDurr**)
- James Gardner, Durrington High School – Experimenting with Subtitling Software (**@langnut**)

- Mel Walton, The Regis School – Pepper Power: How a Dog Can Transform Learning (**@WaltonMel**)
- Ashley Harrold, Blatchington Mill High School – How to Save Time Marking (**@BMS_MrHarrold**)
- Matt McKee, The Shoreham Academy – Developing Independent Learning (**@matt_mckeeSA**)
- Chloe Gardner, Durrington High School – Students As Bloggers (**@ChloeMuriel**)
- Rob Carpenter, Oak Grove College – OpenDyslexic and Target Who (**@djtoadie**)
- David Rogers, Priory School, Southsea – The Art of (Un) Planning: 7 Ideas in 7 Minutes (**@daviderogers**)
- John McKee, Patcham High School – Making Student Voice Meaningful

4. Promoting your TeachMeet

Once you have the presenters lined up, you will need to promote your event to ensure that you get a good attendance. There are a number of ways to do this:

- Send out flyers to surrounding schools and universities (TeachMeets are invaluable for trainee teachers).
- Publicise the event to teachers within your own school.
- Use social media, such as Twitter, Facebook and blogs, to promote your event – be relentless with this and give yourself a good few months to do it.

- Contact local businesses to sponsor your event by providing prizes for a free draw on the night. You will be surprised at their generosity.

- Consider having a high-profile keynote speaker for the event.

5. Other organisational considerations

- Timings – although presentations are scheduled to be seven minutes long, teachers are not great timekeepers, so don't try to squeeze in too many! The optimum number of presentations is about twelve.

- Breaks – schedule in some breaks. This gives you time to catch up if there are any delays in the programme and allows attendees to network and discuss future collaborations.

- Food – as TeachMeets are usually organised as evening events, catering will encourage people to attend. This can be financed either from sponsorship or from your own funds. Another alternative is to contact a local further education establishment and see if their catering students would be interested in providing refreshments.

- IT – make sure you have adequate IT support during the evening. You will be surprised at the number of software compatibility issues you might encounter during the event. For this reason, it is also wise to ask presenters to send you their presentation a week in advance. This gives you the opportunity to check for any compatibility problems.

- Distributing information after the event – so many good ideas can be shared during a TeachMeet that sometimes it can be hard to keep up. So, make sure you plan a way of sharing the presentations after the event. For example:

  - Set up a blog or website where the presentations can be viewed.
  - Record the presentations and then make them available for viewing online (e.g. by setting up a dedicated YouTube account).
  - Produce a summary booklet that can be sent to all attendees.
  - Save the presentations online where they can be easily accessed (e.g. Dropbox).

Evaluation

Teachers on Twitter were asked to finish this sentence: 'TeachMeets are great CPD because ...' Some of their responses included:

- You hear from practicing teachers with ideas that work.
- They bring together the creative and passionate to improve and develop practice to enhance learning.
- I can choose what I want to learn.
- They make me reflect on my own practice.
- Everyone has chosen to be there, so the atmosphere is great and it doesn't feel like a chore.

- They are insightful, entertaining and a great opportunity to network with fellow teachers.
- The ideas are tried and tested and make you reinvent new ideas, keeping your teaching fresh.

Stay connected

- Use the Twitter hashtag **#perfectcpdtm** to publicise your TeachMeets and share your experiences of them.

To-do list

- Choose a date for your TeachMeet. ✓
- Decide whether or not you will approach local businesses to sponsor your event – and approach them if you are. This can help with costs, such as refreshments, and provide prizes for a draw. ✓
- Use the TeachMeet wiki site http://teachmeet. pbworks.com/ for your sign-up stage. ✓
- Ask your teaching staff if anybody is willing to lead a presentation on their work. ✓
- Publicise the event within your own school and to surrounding schools via email and social media sites. ✓

Chapter 10

Lesson Study

Description

Jugyoukenkuu (or 'lesson study' as it is more widely known) is the Japanese art of teacher professional development. It involves the identification of an area of teaching that needs to be developed by a group of teachers. The group then plans a lesson together (the research lesson) to address that area of need, with a particular focus on specific students to monitor their progress. One teacher then delivers the research lesson, while the other members of the group observe. They then interview the target students to gauge their progress and engagement during the lesson. The lesson is then reviewed by the group, with strengths and further areas for development identified. The process is then repeated (with somebody else teaching the research lesson) based on this review.

Implementation

1. Identify your initial group of teachers

A sensible size for a lesson study group is three teachers. This keeps the group manageable and ensures that everyone is actively involved in the process.

In a secondary school setting, there are advantages and dis-advantages to the make-up of the group in terms of subject specialism. By keeping the subject specialism of the teachers the same, you can focus on developing high-quality subject-specific pedagogy. Alternatively, by making the groups cross-curricular, you can transfer good practice from one subject area to another.

It is also worth having a 'lesson study coach' for the group. This is an individual who is not directly involved in the pro-cess, but plays an important role in introducing the group to the process of lesson study, keeping them focused on the method and challenging them to get the best out of it.

2. Identify an area of focus

Once the group of teachers has been identified and the pro-cess explained to them by the coach, they need to decide the focus of the research lesson in terms of the teaching strategy and the target students.

Firstly, they need to identify the research question: what teaching strategy do they want to develop? For example: how can we ensure that we are challenging the more able? How can we effectively assess the progress of students during a lesson, and then use this to promote learning? How can we develop questioning skills to promote deep thinking? How can we ensure that we are engaging the disengaged?

Next, they need to identify three students that the observers will focus on during the research lesson and then interview afterwards. This is a key part of the process, as the progress these students make will be monitored during the research lesson. It is a good idea to pick students with different profiles as this will provide more valuable feedback about the success of the lesson. For example: high ability, middle ability and low ability; currently achieving above, on or below their target level/grade; different 'typical' levels of behaviour/engagement.

At this point, it is also worth discussing and agreeing what questions the students will be asked following the lesson. For example:

- What did you learn during the lesson? How do you know?
- Do you know what you need to do in order to further improve your learning?
- Which aspects of the teaching worked well for you and why?
- How do you think the lesson could be improved? Why?

Clearly the questions will need to be shaped by your initial research question. It is also worth considering at this point how you would expect the students to respond.

3. Group planning of research lesson

The group then sit down and plan the lesson in detail, with a particular focus on addressing the research question and the learning needs of the three focus students.

Once the lesson has been planned, the group should discuss and agree the following:

- Which of the observers will concentrate on each of the focus students during the lesson observation?
- What do you want each of the focus students to be able to do by the end of the lesson?
- What will be the success criteria, if the research question is successfully addressed?

4. Delivery and observation of research lesson

The lesson is then delivered by the member of the group selected, and observed by the other two members – with particular attention given to the focus students. Detailed notes should be taken during the lesson that will relate specifically to the research question and the progress of the focus students.

5. Student interview

As soon as is possible after the lesson, the focus students should be interviewed, using the questions agreed during stage 2 of the process.

6. Review of research lesson

The group then meets to discuss and review the research lesson. Key questions should include:

- To what extent was the research question addressed? How do we know?
- Did the focus students achieve in line with what we had expected, or better, or worse? Why?
- What was the focus students' perception of the lesson? Is this a surprise?
- Overall, what were the successes of the lesson? Why?
- What areas need to be developed further?

7. Next cycle

Having reviewed the initial research lesson and identified areas of teaching that need to be developed further, the next cycle of research lessons is planned. This time it will be delivered by a different member of the group and the research question will be reshaped, based on the development areas from this initial research lesson.

Steps 2–7 will then be repeated, until all members of the group have delivered a research lesson.

8. Dissemination

Once the lesson study process has been completed by the group, they should be given the opportunity to share their findings with their colleagues. This is important because:

- It shares the good practice that will have been developed during the process.
- It shows that the time invested by the teachers is valued.
- It will encourage others to engage with lesson study.

Evaluation

Lesson study works effectively because:

- It encourages teacher collaboration and reflection.
- It allows teachers to take ownership of their own CPD – as they choose the research question they wish to address.
- It is evidence based – as teachers evaluate the teaching methods they are trying to develop.
- It uses student voice to develop the quality of teaching.

Schools should also consider the following points:

- Teachers should be given sufficient time to engage in the process (e.g. planning time, observations).

- Decide whether lesson study will be an optional developmental tool that groups of teachers can choose to do, or whether all staff will be expected to engage with it.

- The role of the coach is essential to the group. They are required to maintain the momentum of the process and to provide sufficient challenge.

- How the findings of each group will be disseminated.

Stay connected

- For further details on lesson study visit http://lessonstudy.co.uk/.

- Follow **@lessonstudyuk** on Twitter.

- Use the Twitter hashtag **#perfectcpdlessonstudy** to share your experiences and resources for lesson study.

To-do list

- Think about how you will provide the time for staff to engage in lesson study. ☑

- Start with a pilot group of teachers to try it out. ☑

- Have an initial training session to go through the process. ☑

- Share the successes of the pilot group with the whole teaching staff. ☑

- Invite the staff to form other lesson study groups. ☑
- Meet regularly with each group to maintain momentum. ☑

Chapter 11
Social Media

Description

Over the last decade, social media such as Twitter, Facebook and blogs have become an established part of our lives – not only at home, but at work too. They allow teachers to discuss and share ideas with thousands of other teachers, all over the world, and at a time that suits them best. They really do act as a global staffroom – without the dirty coffee cups!

Implementation

Twitter

Twitter is rapidly becoming an important source of CPD for teachers. A growing number of teachers and school leaders are now using it to share ideas and resources, discuss issues and initiate a wide range of collaborative projects. I asked a number of teachers who actively use Twitter to give an example of how it has helped them. Here are some of their responses:

- Getting ideas for great resources from other teachers (e.g. whiteboard paint on desks).

- Getting great ideas from other teachers (e.g. SOLO taxonomy as a way to develop student thinking about their learning).

- Networking with other successful departments in other schools.

- Receiving up-to-date information about key issues (e.g. Pupil Premium funding) as it happens from conferences.

- Getting in contact with exam moderators in their subjects – and receiving useful tips.

- Gaining access to a wider network of advanced skills teachers (ASTs) and specialist leaders of education (SLEs) and then working with them.

- Setting up cross-school collaboration projects (e.g. observing IRIS lessons in other schools).

- Getting notifications about updates to the many excellent teacher blogs out there.

- Making contact with business people who are willing to support our students by giving them free books or lead workshops.

- Finding out about forthcoming subject-related events.

- Organising events such as TeachMeets and conferences.

- Arranging visits to other schools.

So, it's worth considering how to get started with Twitter. Here's how you do it:

1. Sign up – go to https://twitter.com/ and register. It's free and all you need is an email address.

2. Your profile – go to your profile page and set up your personal settings, add a bio and include a short piece about what you do (e.g. subject leader in maths at a large comprehensive school on the south coast of England). It is also worth adding a photo of yourself. These two things ensure that other teachers know you are a 'proper' teacher and worth following!

3. Start following – when someone you follow sends a tweet (i.e. writes something on Twitter), it will appear in your timeline. If you are new to Twitter, though, the problem is knowing who to follow. Well, there are thousands of teachers out there, but the following list are worth following to get started:

   Geoff Barton – **@RealGeoffBarton**

   David Didau – **@LearningSpy**

   Zoë Elder – **@fullonlearning**

   Vic Goddard – **@vicgoddard**

   Ross Morrison McGill – **@TeacherToolkit**

   Alex Quigley – **@HuntingEnglish**

   Tom Sherrington – **@headguruteacher**

   John Tomsett – **@johntomsett**

   Dylan Wiliam – **@dylanwiliam**

As you follow these people, you will see who they engage with on Twitter – you may then choose to follow them too.

4. Get involved – as tweets from people you are following appear in your timeline, get involved with the conversations and reply.

5. Use hashtags (#) – a hashtag is a way of 'tagging' a tweet with a particular subject. So, for example, if you write a tweet that you think might be useful to science teachers, you would write **#sciedchat** at the end of your tweet. Then, if anyone searches for **#sciedchat**, your tweet and any others with that hashtag will be filtered in their timeline. You can also use the hashtag in the search bar to look for other teachers in areas of interest (e.g. **#mathsed**, **#pegeeks**). Hashtags are not fixed – anyone can make them up.

6. Chats – there are set times during the week when certain discussions happen on Twitter that might be of interest to teachers or leaders. All you need to do is be on Twitter at that time, search for the hashtag for that particular chat and then get involved. Two popular ones are:

#ukedchat – every Thursday from 8–9 p.m. Covers a range of topics that would be of interest to all teachers.

#sltchat – every Sunday from 8–8.30 p.m. Two topics are discussed each week that would be of interest to school leaders.

Facebook

Facebook is used for CPD to a lesser extent than Twitter, and users tend to set up 'pages' rather than personal accounts. These allow users to share links to other websites and resources and to publicise forthcoming events, such as TeachMeets. It is also used by bloggers to promote their blogs. For example:

https://www.facebook.com/TeacherToolkit

https://www.facebook.com/astsupportaali

To set up a new page, simply scroll down to the bottom of your personal Facebook page and click the 'create page' link. You will then be taken through a series of steps to set up your new CPD page, which will be separate from your personal page.

Blogging

There has been a huge rise in the number of teachers and school leaders who blog about their thoughts and ideas. These are a hugely valuable source of CPD and can be used to share ideas and initiate discussion about key educational topics, as well as enabling teachers and leaders to build their own professional networks. When asked why they blog on Twitter, some common responses from a range of teacher bloggers included:

■ By writing down my thoughts, it encourages me to reflect on my practice.

- Blogging about my practice encourages critique and feedback from peers.
- It's a way of storing good ideas and resources so I don't forget.
- It encourages me to research new teaching methods.
- The thought of influencing teachers and students beyond my own school is appealing.

There are hundreds of educational bloggers, but the following blogs by senior leaders and teachers provide a good starting point.

Blogging head teachers

http://johntomsett.wordpress.com/

http://headguruteacher.com/

John Tomsett and Tom Sherrington are both highly prolific and influential bloggers. They write about their approach to leadership and how this is used to develop teaching and learning across their schools.

Blogging teachers

http://www.learningspy.co.uk/

http://www.huntingenglish.com/

http://fullonlearning.com/

It would be possible to write a book on educational bloggers alone as there are so many of them. But these three, written by David Didau, Alex Quigley and Zoë Elder, respectively, are a great starting place. All of them are great educational thinkers who offer a good mix of their reflections and thoughts about pedagogy, alongside strategies that can be taken straight into the classroom.

There are many more out there. However, if teachers don't have access to them then their usefulness will be limited. The task for the CPD leader is to provide opportunities to share information about blogs with staff and encourage them to engage with the content. Here are a few ideas about how to start:

- Email staff a link to a relevant blog article once a week to share a good idea. For example, this might be linked to a specific developmental area that the school is focusing on at a particular time. Make a list of good blogs available for staff so they don't have to spend hours finding them. There are some suggestions here: http://classteaching.wordpress.com/links/.

- Send out a blog article that relates to a meeting agenda item ahead of the meeting to stimulate thought and discussion (e.g. a blog looking at alternative curriculum models prior to a subject leader meeting where the curriculum is due to be discussed).

- Keep an eye out for blogs that will appeal to a specific group of staff (e.g. subject teams) and then distribute them.

- Point staff to particular blogs at events such as staff meetings and INSET days.

- Set up a 'blog club' – like a book club, but with blogs! Get a group of staff together, circulate a blog for them to read, then meet up in a week's time to discuss the blog and the impact it has had on their practice.

■ Encourage staff to set up their own blog. Those who do usually find it invaluable CPD for themselves as it encourages thinking and reflection about their own practice. It is also a great way to share good practice within a school and, of course, develops networks beyond the school. (One great example of this is from Andy Tharby, an English teacher at my own school: http://reflectingenglish.wordpress.com/.)

It is a fairly straightforward process to set up your own blog. There are a number of free blog providers out there, but two common and easy-to-use ones are http://wordpress.com/ and http://blogger.com/. Once you have set up your blog, it's important to link it to your Twitter account, so that any new post on your blog is then posted in your Twitter timeline. This will encourage your Twitter followers to view, engage with and then share your blog posts.

Evaluation

Undoubtedly, there is huge potential for excellent CPD with social media:

■ It allows you to build up a network of like-minded professionals.

■ It gives you access to a wide range of valuable teaching and/or leadership resources.

- It lets you know what other schools are doing to improve.
- It gives you a wider view on key educational topics and discussion areas.
- It makes it easier to arrange collaborative work and visits to other schools.
- It widens your educational perspective to include a more international dimension.
- The process of writing a blog about your practice is a great reflective tool. It also invites feedback from peers about what you are doing in the classroom.

Some cautionary notes though:

- Tweets and blogs are highly subjective, so be selective with what you read and take on board.
- Most educationalists are very kind and complimentary about their colleagues' tweets or blogs (or ignore them if they don't agree!). However, be prepared for the odd bit of criticism!
- With so many ideas out there, there is the potential to try to implement too many of them. Again, be selective and think about what is going to work in your context.
- Teachers need to be mindful that anything they write in a blog or a tweet is public, so it can be read by parents and students. As this can be linked directly back to the school, we need to think very carefully about what we write and how it could be interpreted by others. If in doubt, check with your head teacher.

■ Safeguarding is a very important issue that will need to be discussed and resolved by each school. The key questions to examine are what measures your school needs to put in place to ensure that staff can use social media as a valuable CPD resource, while not compromising their own integrity or the school's, and how to ensure that students are not placed in potentially harmful situations.

Stay connected

■ Follow **@shaun_allison** on Twitter and share how you have implemented effective CPD at your school, using the hashtag **#perfectcpd**.

■ If you set up a new blog, publicise it on Twitter using the hashtag **#perfectcpdblog**.

■ Leave your thoughts and reflections on the articles that appear at http://classteaching.wordpress.com/.

To-do list

■ Sign up to Twitter. ☑

■ Start reading some of the educational blogs mentioned in this chapter. ☑

■ Start following the educational tweeters listed in this chapter. ☑

- Contribute to conversations and organised chats (e.g. **#sltchat**). ✓
- Decide on a topic you could blog about and set up your own blog. ✓
- Use Twitter to publicise your blog. ✓

Chapter 12
Student-Led CPD

Description

There is a great deal of discussion, both positive and negative, about the usefulness of the 'student voice' in schools. At one extreme are those who believe that it offers little of value to teachers and school leaders. People who hold this view argue that it is teachers who have the teaching expertise, and as students do not, they should not be telling teachers how to do their job. At the other extreme are those who suggest that as students experience nearly 1,000 lessons every year, they are well placed to tell us what works and what doesn't in terms of their learning.

If you fall into the first camp, this chapter may be of limited interest to you. If, however, you feel that we should listen to students' experiences and reflections about their learning, and then use this to inform our teaching through student-led CPD, then please read on!

Implementation

Student-led learning walks

The physical learning environment of the classroom can have a huge impact on student learning. With this in mind, a good strategy is to gather together a group of students and ask them to take teachers on a tour around the school (usually best done after school) and point out features in classrooms that have a positive (or negative) impact on their learning.

Some of the things they are likely to point out include:

- They like a neat, tidy and well-organised room, so they know where exercise books, textbooks, graph paper, etc. are stored.

- 'Prompt posters' are useful and allow them to work with greater independence (e.g. exam techniques, connectives lists, question command words).

- Having assessment criteria displayed around the room is useful as it allows students to plan their own improvements.

- Examples of excellent work displayed around the room is invaluable. It serves as a great inspiration to students and shows them what standard they should aspire to.

- Displaying subject-specific keywords is useful as this helps students when they are responding to questions.

Student question-and-answer panels

Student panels can be set up easily. Gather together a group of students along with some staff who can then quiz students about their views on a particular aspect of teaching. It is quite useful to have a specific focus for each discussion.

For example, following up on the learning environment theme, to the question, 'Does the classroom learning environment make a difference to your learning?', the students said:

- Messy rooms are distracting.
- Boring classrooms mean boring lessons.
- Colourful displays can be inspiring.
- We're more likely to get things done in a comfortable environment.
- Pictures and keywords help us to engage.
- You learn from examples of good work.

In response to the question, 'Do you think classroom layout has an effect on your learning?', the students said:

- The layout needs changing more.
- Grouping tables together encourages group work.
- We hate it when we're not facing the front in groups.
- The horseshoe arrangement of desks is good for discussion.
- Naughty students sat with good students helps them to work – they are good role models.

Student feedback on pedagogical development

As schools look to improve and develop the quality of teaching, it is worth soliciting the views of students as a contribution to the overall discussion. For example, if the school has identified certain aspects of pedagogy that it is looking to develop, get a group of students together and ask them what they think works in these areas.

Students came up with the following points when they were asked about these four topics:

Questioning

- Ask us questions that make us think.
- Follow up questions with more questions, which will make us think more deeply.
- Get more students involved by using strategies like lolly sticks with student names on.
- If someone says 'I don't know' in response to a question, don't let them get away with not answering.

Feedback

- After a test or piece of writing, instead of just putting a tick or a 'well done', tell us specifically what was good about it, so we know to do more of it.
- Tell us what to do to improve, but not in long paragraphs. This makes it hard to pick out what to do.
- Talk to us about our work, so we can ask specific questions about what to do to improve.

Independence

- Before we are sent off to work on a task independently, the teacher needs to explain to us thoroughly the idea we are working on, otherwise we won't be able to do it well.

- Don't sit us next to our friends, as we are less likely to work independently.

- Keep checking our work if we are working independently – if we are getting it wrong, we won't know.

Challenge

- One of the best ways to make sure we are challenged is to keep asking lots of difficult questions which will make us think.

- Make sure there is always some kind of interesting extension work. Not more of the same work, but different and harder.

- Don't give students the choice of work, depending on their ability, as most will just pick the easy work.

Now, some teachers would argue that these comments are not telling us anything new, so it's not a particularly useful exercise. This may well be the case – students often point out the obvious – but sometimes these are the very points that we lose sight of (e.g. to develop independence, to make sure we explain tasks fully in the first place). This draws attention to the importance of modelling in our pedagogy toolbox. Furthermore, gathering students together in this kind of forum allows us to question them more deeply about their thoughts with regard to effective teaching and learning.

Student–teacher co-construction of learning

The most pure form of student-led CPD is where students and teachers plan the learning together. There are a number of ways doing this, such as:

- Scheme of work development – students are given a copy of the scheme of work and are asked to review it. This includes looking at the planned activities and making alternative suggestions based on what they think will work in terms of their own learning. This can be done before the topic is taught or after as a review, or both.

- Peer teaching – groups of students are given a topic to teach to their peers. This can be carried out on different scales. It might lead to a small group of students teaching a particular aspect of a lesson, or even a whole lesson, to a class. On a bigger scale, the entire scheme of work could be distributed between the students in a class, and a small group (perhaps three or four students) are then given the responsibility for teaching their allocated aspect of the scheme of work to the rest of the class.

- Lesson planning – teachers are allocated individual students who they work alongside to plan a lesson together. This can be further developed by the student then observing the co-planned lesson and feeding back to the teacher. This could be done on a voluntary basis or as a whole focus on an INSET day.

Evaluation

There are many benefits to student-led CPD:

- It has the potential to be hugely empowering for students and enlightening for teachers.
- Clearly, there are some sensitivities to consider when teachers and students work together. Therefore, it is usually best to implement these strategies on a voluntary basis for those teachers who would like to try it out. As success grows with this initial trial group, it can then be widened to other staff.
- Consider how student-led findings will be shared with the wider staff – INSET days, school blogs and staff meetings are all good ways of doing this.

Stay connected

- Share your experiences of student-led CPD using the Twitter hashtag **#perfectcpdstudent**.

To-do list

- Decide what you want students to help you to achieve (e.g. getting their views on what helps them learn, using them to co-plan lessons, using them to observe lessons). ✓

- If one doesn't already exist, set up a group of students you can work with. ✓

- Spend some time discussing with the students how to carry out their role. ✓

- If their role will include working with teachers, find some staff volunteers for them to work with first. ✓

- Share the successes of the trial with the rest of the teaching staff and use this to widen participation in the project. ✓

Chapter 13

Next Steps

Having read this book, there are some key questions that CPD leaders now need to consider and then act on.

1. Focus: What do we want our CPD programme to achieve?

This question should address two primary points:

1. Enabling our teachers to plan, deliver and then evaluate the best possible lessons they can, on a day-in, day-out basis, in order to achieve the best possible learning for our students.

2. Enabling our leaders to be aware of and then reduce variability within their teams.

If your CPD programme addresses these two points, it is likely to have a significant impact on school improvement. Arguably, these should be at the heart of any school's core purpose.

Next, your CPD programme will need to be put into the context of your school, so you will need to come up with some specific development points on which to focus. For example:

- What aspects of teaching are we good at? What areas do we need to develop more?
- Do we have a collective understanding of what great teaching looks like?
- Who are our strongest teachers and how can we use them to develop our weakest teachers?
- Which teams within the school have the greatest degree of variability, and what has already been put in place to address this?

2. Current CPD practice: What do we currently do in terms of CPD that works well and not so well?

It is very important to reflect on what you currently do in terms of CPD, then keep what works well and stop doing what doesn't. How can you assess the impact of CPD? With great difficulty, unfortunately, as teaching is such a complex skill and so many factors affect it. However, if the purpose of CPD is to improve the quality of teaching, and the purpose of teaching is to produce confident and competent learners who then go on to achieve well, it would be worth looking at:

- Quality of teaching evidence – whether that is through lesson observations, learning walks, peer observations, work scrutiny, etc.
- Student voice – how confident do students feel about their learning?
- Teacher voice – how are teachers feeling about their teaching? Are they enjoying it? Are they feeling inspired to try new things? Do they feel a sense of ownership over their own development? Do they feel they work within a supportive framework?
- Assessment data – a core purpose of schools is to make sure students achieve well in assessments/exams, etc.

3. Developing your CPD provision: What can we introduce with respect to CPD, and how?

Having identified what you already do well with regard to CPD and stripped away what doesn't work, you can now consider which of the strategies in this book you are going to implement.

Caution is needed here. If you try to implement too much too soon, you will risk diluting the effectiveness of the strategies and fail to address any of your issues successfully. It is better to consider your CPD programme over a longer period, say three years, and implement a few new strategies each

Target staff: teachers/middle leaders/senior leaders

Year	Development points to address	CPD strategies to support development points	Success criteria	Monitoring and impact
1				
2				
3				

year, with a view to addressing a small number of development points well each year. A three-year CPD plan, like the one below, is a good way of crystallising your thoughts.

When planning your CPD programme, it is really important to think about your own school context. As a CPD coordinator, you will know which strategies should work and which ones might be a challenge. That isn't to say these strategies should be ignored, but perhaps put off to a later year and planned for gradually. For example, if there hasn't been much collaborative CPD in your school, you might wish to start off in year one with a more structured approach, such as learning development groups (see Chapter 4) before moving on to 'looser' CPD strategies, such as coaching (see Chapter 3) in year two. In year three, this could then be developed further, using something like lesson study (see Chapter 10).

Optional CPD activities, such as 15 minute forums (see Chapter 2), can and should be implemented as soon as possible, as they are a great way of building a culture of sharing and collaboration across a school.

4. Review and reflect: How are we going to know what we are doing is working and what will we do about it?

In the planning stage, think carefully about the success criteria you will use (see point 2 above) to check the impact of the CPD strategies you are intending to implement. Be mindful of the fact that change in schools can sometimes appear to get off to a great start, but then drift off course. A key role of the CPD leader is to use their judgement to keep the momentum going, while not over-burdening staff during those 'difficult times'. This is a fine balancing act. Don't be afraid of changing direction if, after having a good shot at a particular strategy, the impact appears to be limited.

5. Stay connected

Social media, such as Twitter, allow educationalists now, more than ever before, to share what works well and to collaborate with teachers and schools all over the world.

Leading CPD in a school is a highly rewarding and important job. Hopefully, this book has inspired you to try out some new things – so share your successes using the hashtag **#perfectcpd**.

Good luck!

Wider Reading

Allison, S. and Harbour, M. (2009). *The Coaching Toolkit: A Practical Guide For Your School*. London: SAGE Publications.

Beere, J. and Broughton, T. (2013). *The Perfect Teacher Coach*. Carmarthen: Independent Thinking Press.

Berger, R. (2003). *An Ethic of Excellence: Building a Culture of Craftsmanship With Students*. Portsmouth, NH: Heinemann.

Bubb, S. and Earley, P. (2007). *Leading and Managing Continuing Professional Development: Developing People, Developing Schools*. London: SAGE Publications.

Bubb, S. and Earley, P. (2010). *Helping Staff Develop in Schools*. London: SAGE Publications.

Dweck, C. (2006). *Mindset: How You Can Fulfil Your Potential*. London: Constable & Robinson.

Earley, P. and Porritt, V. (eds) (2009). *Effective Practices in Continuing Professional Development: Lessons from Schools*. London: Institute of Education, University of London.

Fullan, M. (2008). *The Six Secrets of Change*. San Francisco, CA: Jossey-Bass.

Gladwell, M. (2008). *Outliers: The Story of Success*. New York: Little, Brown and Company.

Hattie, J. (2009). *Visible Learning: A Synthesis of Over 800 Meta-Analyses Relating to Achievement*. London: Routledge.

Heath, C. and Heath, D. (2011). *Switch: How to Change Things When Change is Hard*. New York: Random House.

Kelly, S. (2006). *The CPD Coordinator's Toolkit*. London: SAGE Publications.

Lemov, D. (2010). *Teach Like a Champion: 49 Techniques That Put Students on the Path to College*. San Francisco, CA: Jossey-Bass.

Ofsted (2010). *Good Professional Development in Schools: How Does Leadership Contribute?* Ref: 080254. Available at: <http://www.ofsted.gov.uk/resources/good-professional-development-schools>

Ofsted (2014). *School Inspection Handbook*. Ref: 120101. Available at: <www.ofsted.gov.uk/resources/school-inspection-handbook>

Smith, A. (2011). *High Performers: The Secrets of Successful Schools*. Carmarthen: Crown House Publishing.

Strong, R. (2012). A Study to Evaluate the Effectiveness of Differentiation Strategies within the Secondary Classroom, *Class Teaching*. Available at: <http://classteaching.wordpress.com/learning-innovator-reports/>

Trignano, S. (2013). SOLO Taxonomy, *Class Teaching*. Available at: <http://classteaching.wordpress.com/learning-innovator-reports/>

Wiliam, D. (2010). Teacher Quality: How To Get More Of It. Speech delivered at the Spectator Schools Revolution Conference, London, March.

Wolstenholme, L. (2013). Using ICT to Enhance Teaching and Learning, *Class Teaching*. Available at: <http://classteaching.wordpress.com/learning-innovator-reports/>

978-178135103-1

978-178135003-4

978-178135002-7

www.independentthinkingpress.com